God Worthy?

A Short Course in Christianity

PRESSED
THOUGHTS

GOD WORTHY?

A Short Course in Christianity

2nd Edition

© 2014-2020 Ted LaFemina

Printed in the United States of America

ALL RIGHTS RESERVED

Published by Pressed Thoughts LLC

www.pressedthoughts.com

42

ISBN 978-0-9850102-8-7

DEDICATION

This book is dedicated to anyone who is reflecting on the fact that God is not an integral part of their lives, wondering if He exists at all, or if so, should they allow Him in, given all the pains of the world. For those who don't know if they are worthy of God's tender mercy, and for those that simply don't know what to do next. Especially veterans who have suffered the horrors of conflict and the incarcerated men, women, and children who may feel discarded from society and who wonder if God has any place for them at all.

CONTENTS

INTRODUCTION

Over the years, I've had many conversations as I've sought to understand my own faith and to understand other people's view of God. Some, when asked about God, echo Pierre-Simon Laplace's famous words: *I have no need of that hypothesis.* Others recognize that God exists, but do not know how to make room for him in their lives, and still others shared words with me that were more difficult to hear:

You don't know my past. I've done too much to be right with God.

I've seen too much evil in the world to believe in God.

If God doesn't want anything to do with me, then I don't want anything to do with him.

As I listened to these people share their life and their views, it became apparent that each of their lives is shaped by a steady undercurrent of discontent as they strive to find joy and a meaningful purpose.

When something painful happens to us, either physically or emotionally, our immediate reaction is to get away from whatever is causing us that pain. A strange thing happens to us, though, if we are afflicted over and over and can't find a way to avoid the pain: we begin to learn to live with it. In fact, we begin to believe that the pain is just part of life—just part of how we are meant to live. Psychologists call this *learned helplessness*. They found that once we have become accustomed to living with pain, then we stop looking for a way out of it. As a result, our lives become a drudge—we plod along with occasional moments of excitement, more than occasional moments of stress, weariness, or depression, and we may begin to view life more as something to endure rather than the precious gift it is meant to be. Some are keenly aware of this drain on our souls, while others experience this undercurrent of discontent as the nagging feeling that something is absent … as if the last puzzle piece of life was somehow missing from the box.

Many of us first learned about God at an early age. We may have been dragged to church and forced to sit on hard pews as a priest or pastor droned on and on. We may have been threatened with God by over-righteous relatives: *He's watching you, so you better straighten up!* Or we may have only heard of God through television or neighbors who mentioned that they went to church every Sunday.

As I've talked with people over the years, what I've found is that few of us have a clear understanding of God and what it means to have a relationship with him. Even those who've studied diligently in Bible Study groups, or even in seminary, can miss the idea of a relationship amidst the noise of theological doctrines, memorized scripture verses, and church ceremony.

In the three and one-half years of his ministry, Jesus' most impactful teaching wasn't done with scriptural exposition (which he did do), it was done with tears, laugher, and caring.

The comedian John Mulaney joked that Christ's greatest miracle was the fact that Jesus, a man in his thirties, went out and made twelve new friends. I'm not sure that

God Worthy?

John quite understood the significance of his own insight. Over and over again, the scriptures show that his disciples, while they walked with Jesus, didn't quite understand his parables (see Mark 4:13), and they didn't understand the significance of the scriptures (see Luke 24), but they did understand that Jesus cared for them when he wept (John 11:35). These twelve men that Jesus befriended were a diverse bunch, and many would have been natural enemies of each other. Simon was a Zealot, a member of a group that was willing to use terrorism to drive out the Romans. Matthew had sold out to the Romans, buying his way into the job of tax-collector for this occupying nation. Peter and several others were simple fisherman and farmers, but John and his brother James were members of a family that appear to be aggressive social climbers.

Jesus taught these men how to appreciate each other and love each other in spite of their fears, faults, and failures. He taught them how to love and be loved, how to serve and be served. And most of all, he taught them how to have this same close relationship with him by bringing them into his own relationship with his father, God Almighty.

So much of the frustration, disappointment, and emptiness of life evaporates away as a person comes to know the true Lord as he is. If you choose to get to know God, you can expect feelings such as these to be replaced with a sense of purpose, acceptance, love, and joy. You can also expect the quality of the relationships with those around you to grow and deepen. The problems of life do not disappear, of course, but their impact on our well-being is changed.

The first thing that everyone should learn about God is that he gives us choices. In order to get to know God better, we must make the choice to know God better. If you don't know God now, then your life has some form of emptiness to it—some form of persistent pain and suffering that you have come to believe is an inevitable part of your existence. This book is intended to help you understand that you have an open door—a way out of a sense of help-lessness that you may not have realized you have.

The title of this book, *God Worthy?*, is meant to be taken in three ways. First, is God worthy of you? Is he nice enough, fair enough, or smart enough to be worthy of your friendship and trust? Second, are you worthy of God? Are you good enough to be acceptable to him—good enough for him to want a relationship with you? Finally, what does it mean to live a life that is worthy of God?

But is it OK to come to God with such questions? Is it wise to question whether or not God is worthy of you? In November of 1978, a cult leader named Jim Jones murdered nearly all of his followers, over nine hundred people—two hundred of which were children. Just as it would have been wise for those who worshiped Jim Jones to investigate his character before placing their faith in him, so it is wise to seek a better understanding of God's character before placing our faith in the Lord. God is not only OK with this sort of investigation, he has gone to great lengths to provide us the means to arrive at an answer. In Matthew 11:28, Jesus gives us an invitation: *Come to me, all who labor and are heavy laden, and I will give you rest.* God understands that providing answers to our questions helps to develop the trust necessary for us to accept this invitation. God is not threatened by the questions we bring to him, nor is he angry and resentful. In fact, he welcomes the conversation and wants us to come to him as we are.

The challenge with these questions is that simple academic answers provide no satisfaction. Just as a description of what it feels like to ride a bike can never capture the experience of actually riding a bike, a description of what it means to live in a relationship with God can never capture the profoundness of the experience. Therefore, the remainder of this book is not structured to provide straightforward academic answers, but rather is designed to be a short course in Christianity, sharing the way Jesus shared, helping you to look at yourself, at others, and at God from his perspective. By doing so, it will reveal to you a practical idea of what it means to live life on the other side of that door, a life with a God that is the source of all hope, joy, and love.

ARE YOU GOOD ENOUGH FOR GOD?

Are you worthy of God? Are you good enough? Ask any group of people and you will likely get answers that fall into one of the following three categories. The first is those who will tell you they are generally good people, and they may also tell you how they give to charitable causes and are nice to those they meet. The second is those who will tell you they aren't good enough, that they've done too many things in the past to be right with God. Finally, the third will reject the question altogether because they cannot accept the idea of anyone setting a standard for their life.

The question is a penetrating one because we all have an internal craving to be accepted and, at a deeper level, to be loved. This craving for acceptance is so powerful that it directly, or indirectly, influences most of the key decisions in our lives. Countless stories abound of high achievers who propel themselves forward in a vain attempt to gain the acceptance of their fathers. Other stories are those of women who stick by abusive husbands because, in some strange way, these men make them feel like they belong or are unworthy of love.

In the book, *Searching for God Knows What*, Donald Miller, commenting on the story of Genesis, explains that in the Garden of Eden before the fall we had a close relationship with God and that our sense of security, purpose, and acceptance came through this relationship. Once Adam and Eve stopped trusting in God, this relationship was broken, and we lost our sense of acceptance. Thus, the idea of whether or not we are good enough for God is really about acceptance—that ultimate, fulfilling acceptance of knowing that God knows us and loves us and that our lives do have meaning and purpose.

The question, though, pre-supposes that God has a threshold, a minimum standard that must be met. When pressed to explain what this minimum standard is, those who had told you they are good enough for God will often describe the standard as being just a little below where they are now, while those who think they are not good enough will describe the standard as being somewhere out of reach.

Many who reject God altogether do so not because they don't want God's love, but rather, they find it easier to reject the idea of God than to accept the idea that they may be unacceptable. I was talking with a father who had two daughters born one year apart. Both started playing soccer when they were six, and both enjoyed the game for several seasons. However, by the third grade, the younger daughter began to realize that she would never play at the level of her sister (who was, perpetually, one year ahead of her). Rather than continue in the game she enjoyed, she announced one day that she no longer liked soccer. It was easier to reject the sport, then to accept the idea of being unacceptable.

These views on God's requirements for acceptance are flawed and leave us at risk to succumb to spirits of judgementalism or hopelessness. Neither bring people into the kind of relationship with God that can be truly fulfilling. The reason we may find the answer to this question of being good enough so elusive is that we fail to take the time to look for the answer from God's worldview, the worldview he shares with us through the pages of the Bible.

If you kneeled down before God and asked: *Well, Lord, am I good enough?* He would likely tell you that now is not the time to ask that question, as 1 Corinthians 4:5 tells us: *do not pronounce judgment before the time, before the Lord comes, who will bring to light the things now hidden in darkness and will disclose the purposes of the heart.* Rather than ask God if you are good enough, it is more productive to ask yourself these two important questions: *Do I want to be good enough?* and, if so, *Am I willing to let God be my life coach?*

The first of these question is, in essence, asking if you want a restored relationship with God, if you want to be accepted by God. The second of these is asking if you are willing to accept God yourself. Willing to trust that he does care about and want the best for you, and willing to allow him to mold you, using whatever path he chooses. If you were to answer *yes* to both these questions, then what would happen next? What would you have to *do*?

There has been a long-running debate on what you have to *do* to be acceptable to God. Some say that the only requirement is to have faith, as espoused by Paul in Romans 3:28: *For we hold that one is justified by faith apart from works of the law.* Others say that you have to do good works as explained by James (v. 2:24) *You see that a person is justified by works and not by faith alone.*

I pondered this question at a time when the winter Olympics games were taking place in Sochi, Russia and wondered if a reporter were to ask *When someone tries out and wins a spot on an Olympic ski team, do they have to ski?* That is, if they just enjoyed the experience of being on an Olympic team and the thrill of walking around the Olympic village wearing their official uniform, but they really didn't feel like skiing, would they have to ski anyway?

You would probably not attempt to answer the question, and instead tell the reporter that the question itself is ridiculous. No one who didn't want to ski would ever bother to try out for the team, so the question itself is a non-issue.

In the same way, when a person puts their faith in Christ, they are declaring their desire to be like him, their desire to know him better, and their desire to love like him. Any question about a Christian *having* to do good works is as ridiculous as the question about the Olympic skier having to ski.

In childhood, our parents constantly taught us to behave well. I remember many times being reprimanded for fighting with my siblings, and I still remember that distinctive taste of Ivory® soap that I experienced when I didn't realize my mother was in earshot as I experimented with some newly acquired vocabulary. We have all heard the Ten Commandments and most think that the Bible teaches us to be good, but the surprising revelation you get when you study the Bible is that Jesus was more interested in the *attitude of our thoughts* than our *behavior*. In Matthew 5:21-22 he says *You have heard that it was said to those of old, "You shall not murder; and whoever murders will be liable to judgment." But I say to you that everyone who is angry with his brother will be liable to judgment.* And in vv. 5:27-28, *You have heard that it was said, "You shall not commit adultery." But I say to you that everyone who looks at a woman with lustful intent has already committed adultery with her in his heart.* It's not that Jesus doesn't care about what we do, it is that he knows that our brokenness is in our hearts and that any sinful actions we take are simply the physical manifestations of our broken thoughts.

So what do you have to do once you've joined God's team, when you put your faith in Jesus? You need to change your heart. This, ultimately, is the purpose of God's saving grace, but it does not happen automatically; it requires your continuous participation.

God Worthy?

So where do you begin? The first thing an athlete does when joining an Olympic team is to work with their coach to prepare a comprehensive training plan that will help them attain the condition and skill they will need to compete. Step one in developing this plan is to perform an honest self-evaluation, an evaluation that is conducted without fear. This same process is true when joining God's team.

If you have never done so, set aside a block of quiet time to look back objectively on your life, through God's eyes. Spend time considering what your life's priorities should be for you to be the kind of man or women you were created to be. Then reflect on what your life's priorities have actually been, that is, how you have actually spent your time and money and the choices you've made up to this point in life.

For some, the critical choices that have set the pattern of their lives were made in youth. Research done at the National Institutes of Health has shown that the part of the brain that makes risk-based decisions isn't fully formed until about the age of twenty-six. Prior to that age, we are prone to make choices that are reactionary–driven by emotions and concerns about what our friends may think of us. Through much of man's history, societies built strong family and community structures to guide young men and women during these critical years, but unfortunately, in today's world many of those structures have disappeared. The result is that many of us continue to have our lives defined, at least partially, by the consequences of choices made in youth, and so when looking back objectively, we may find that our day to day focus has been more about survival–living life day by day, gravitating toward short-term distractions to pass the time rather than growing towards our priorities.

Daniel Howard was one such man whose choices soon landed him in prison where he died at the age of thirty two. But before he died, and while still in prison, Daniel became a hero and inspiration to hundreds both inside and outside the institution where he lived. Daniel, after spending time reflecting on his past choices, recognized that the world was full of injustices and always will be if for no other reason than the fact that societies can never quite agree on what constitutes justice. However, he also recognized that the world was full of opportunities and within the prison walls, began encouraging his fellow inmates to *stop doing time, and start using time!*

He shared, with all who would listen, the importance of responding with thoughtfulness to both the opportunities and injustices by considering carefully how our response may impact the future lives of both ourselves and others and how the cumulative effect of our day to day choices should align with our life goals and priorities. Reacting without thought, he found, rarely leads us to where we want to go in life, and waiting on the world to change, waiting for others to remove the injustices of life before we move forward, will lead us only to frustration.

Daniel's mantra recognized that we can feel trapped in the life created by our choices, but then recognized that while we still breath, we can use our own initiative to uncover, create, and leverage opportunities to change that life and steer it in a new direction.

When piloting a boat on a lake in thick fog, it is difficult to know what direction you have been steering, but by looking backwards at the wake you have created, you can easily see when you are arcing left or right. This analogy holds for life. To help understand how to steer it in a new direction, you have to periodically, turn around and look behind.

Once you've reflected on your life's priorities, look behind and review the things you have done, or that you have avoided doing, that have been hurtful to others; things that you did for selfish reasons, for greed, or for pride. Think also on the attitudes that you have held towards others. Have you harbored anger, hatred, resentment, or jealousy? Have you chosen simply not to care about others at all? Have you cared for others but never expressed that caring in a tangible way? As you build this list, you may regret the things that you have done or failed to do, but while it is counter-productive to punish yourself over past decisions, it is important to own up to the choices you have made and take responsibility for their impact.

Next, take the time to review the hurtful things that others have done to you and the feelings that you have toward them. Consider both individuals who have harmed you and the injustices wrought by society as a whole.

In Romans 3:23, the Apostle Paul tells us that *all have sinned and fall short of the glory of God*. Paul didn't choose the word *all* lightly, because it is important to understand that everyone who comes to God, comes holding a list of their past failings and shortcomings. It is also important to understand that this word *all* includes those that have sinned against you. Jesus told the parable of the prodigal son (Luke 15:11-32) because he wants us to understand that, not only is he willing to forgive and forget all your past sins, he is overjoyed that you are coming back to him. However, *coming back to him* means something. It means you want to come into a community ruled by a spirit of love and forgiveness. This implies that you yourself must learn to forgive. In Matthew 6:14-15, Jesus said *if you forgive others their trespasses, your heavenly Father will also forgive you, but if you do not forgive others their trespasses, neither will your Father forgive your trespasses*, and in Matthew 5:7 *Blessed are the merciful, for they shall receive mercy.*

God is willing, even eager, to forgive all the past sins you've listed, and he is also willing to forgive the sinful attitudes that you still hold in your heart at this moment. In order to enter into his community, however, you need to be willing to show the same kind of compassion and mercy that comes from forgiveness that God is extending to you. The original Greek word, translated as *blessed* in Matthew 5:7, is *makarios*, which means *happy*, but not happy as in *I'm happy the commercial is over*, but rather a transcendic happy, as in *I'm happy to hold my baby for the first time*. Ever thought about why God would be eager to forgive you? It's because having a restored relationship with you would make him happy. It's a remarkable thought, isn't it? But this restoration cannot happen until you learn to forgive.

So why do we have such difficulty forgiving the people who hurt us? Why do we not always feel this transcendic happiness when we do muster up the courage to forgive? It is because we do not yet have the heart of Christ; we do not yet view those who hurt us with the same sense of compassion that Jesus has for us.

Once you come to realize that you have sinned, that you have hurt others, and that you admit that you yourself made the selfish decisions to do the things that you have done, and once you have a desire to change your ways and be more like Christ, then Jesus will accept you onto his team. Jesus tells us in Matthew 5:3: *Blessed are the poor in spirit, for theirs is the kingdom of heaven* and then in 5:6 he continues with *Blessed are those who hunger and thirst for righteousness, for they shall be satisfied*. Being *poor in spirit* means that you understand and acknowledge the sinful attitudes of your heart and being one that has a *hunger and thirst for righteousness* refers to your having a strong desire to have the heart of God; to be someone who truly loves all those around them. God promises us that, as we develop this kind of heart, our sense of happiness will increase, we will come to feel the love and acceptance of God, and we will begin to experience *the peace of God, which surpasses all understanding* (Philippians 4:7).

Wouldn't it be easy if God would just change our hearts instantly when we first turn back toward him? This is not, however, the plan God lays out for us in the Scriptures. The Scriptures tell us that our transformation will be a process. As we read through the Gospels and the letters of the New Testament, we find them guiding us and encouraging us to do those things that will help us change our hearts.

Frequently the New Testament extols us to *repent*, a word whose meaning is often misunderstood. The Greek word translated as *repent*, *metanoeo*, doesn't mean *to say you're sorry*, it means *to change one's mind*–which is a process. In Romans 12:2, Paul admonishes us with *Do not be conformed to this world, but be transformed by the renewal of your mind, that by testing you may discern what is the will of God, what is good and acceptable and perfect* and again in 1 Corinthians 3:18 he exclaims *we all, with unveiled face, beholding the glory of the Lord, are being transformed into the same image from one degree of glory to another. For this comes from the Lord who is the Spirit.* From these passages and others, we can see that not only is changing our heart and mind a process, it is both something that we must do and something that comes from the Lord.

The chapters that follow are designed to help you to participate in this transformational process, designed to help you change your heart and mind. Understand, though, that God does not have repeatable, formulaic processes to transform your heart; rather, this change comes through your growing relationship with him. Understand also that God has no desire to change *you*; that is, to change who you are–he made you who you are and, in fact, made you in his own image. The transformation he talks about isn't about *changing* you; it is really about *freeing* you.

As you continue reading, you may come to understand that stumbling blocks to faith need to be overcome, and areas of your life will need cultivation to enable your faith to bloom. God isn't expecting you to be a superstar in every aspect of life; he simply expects you to seek to grow, to seek to know his heart better. It is likely that you have already begun this journey, and it is also likely that the process has had its share of starts and stops, periods when your faith has filled you with joy and periods when your spirit life has seemed flat. Realize that every great surgeon and every master architect started school as a child. Each day, they learned a little more and grew a little more. They picked their nose, spilled their milk, and lost their homework–and yet, by never giving up, by stretching just a little more each day, they became masters of healing and great change. As you continue on, take the time to read through the pages that follow with a pencil in hand. Highlight passages that strike a chord and make notes about passages that prompt you to think. Allow the process of reading and pondering to stretch you just a little more each day and to refocus your journey towards the heart of God. I have no doubt that, as you proceed on this journey, a day will come when you wake up to find that you are becoming a master healer and, with God's guidance, one who affects great change.

ACCEPT GOD'S GRACE

What if you have done things that are so bad that God can never forgive you? *Father, forgive them, for they know not what they do* were the words that Jesus cried out while hanging on the cross (Luke 23:34). These people had whipped him till his flesh fell off his back, tormented him and laughed at him as they pounded a crown of thorns into his head, spat on him, pounded two huge spikes into his hands, and then a third through his heel in such a way as to maximize the agony and prolong his life so that he could further experience that agony. Then, right in front of Jesus' friends and family, they argued over which one of them got to keep his clothes, as if his body meant nothing more to them than a hangar at a secondhand clothing shop. Breathing while hanging from a Roman cross was excruciating, yet Jesus was determined that he would muster enough breath to utter those words of forgiveness. The Romans soldiers *knew* how to extract the most pain and humiliation from a person when they killed them, and they repeated this exercise frequently. These same soldiers crucified two others that day and almost certainly crucified other unfortunates on a regular basis. What Jesus meant, when he said *they know not what they do*, is that their hearts and minds were so clouded with the sinfulness of this world that they didn't know how much God loved them, they didn't know how far God was willing to go to redeem them, nor did they know what having a heart of love could mean to them. The truth is, there is nothing that you could have done for which God will not forgive you. Nothing.

Shortly before the end of the cold war between the Soviet Union and America, the movie *Moscow on the Hudson* came out. The film contained a scene showing a recently defected Russian looking in a grocery store for the coffee line. When someone directed him to the coffee aisle he nearly had a nervous breakdown as he scanned shelf after shelf of this dry roasted manna. Growing up in a country starved of luxuries, and even starved of many necessities, made it difficult for his mind to comprehend the idea that, in this other world, something like coffee was readily available, with no long lines and in a multitude of varieties.

Likewise, when you grow up in an environment in which love is not a part of life, in which everyone selfishly fends for themselves, it can be difficult to step into the Kingdom of God in which love is expressed in so many varieties. In the movie, it took a long time for this émigré, portrayed by Robin Williams, to adapt to this new world, but the challenge wasn't that the coffee wasn't available. It was—the grocery store was always available to him. In this same way, the forgiveness and love of God is available to you, and God is especially anxious for you to accept it. It is OK if it takes some time to accept his forgiveness, but understand that not only is God's forgiveness final and complete, it is also intended to serve a purpose. This purpose is to start you on a new life with him. In Philippians 3:13, Paul, who struggled for a time with his own guilt, said *Brothers, I do not consider that I have made it my own. But one thing I do: forgetting what lies behind and straining forward to what lies ahead.* The longer you hold on to your guilt and regrets, reliving the mistakes of your past, and the longer you are holding God at arm's length, the longer you are delaying the purpose for which God created you.

I was with my friend, Jim, when he received a letter from his daughter. Jim and his wife have huge hearts and years earlier had adopted a troubled teenager. As you might expect, the experience had its challenges. This teenager was now grown and just had her first baby. In the letter, she shared that she could never understand how Jim and his wife could love her; never, that is, until she held her own baby in her arms. The first time she ever fully experienced true unconditional love was when she felt it for her own baby. In that moment, she suddenly understood the love that had been given to her by Jim and his wife. Many view Jesus' words *if you forgive others their trespasses, your heavenly Father will also forgive you* as an implied threat, but this view doesn't fully appreciate the extent of God's understanding of our hearts. While it can be difficult to love if you have never received love, it can also be difficult to accept love until you extend love. God's commands to extend mercy, compassion, and forgiveness to others are intended to be more than an encouragement to be holy; they are a means by which we can fully understand God's love for us. As Paul exclaimed, in Romans 11:33, *Oh, the depth of the riches and wisdom and knowledge of God!*

If you find that you understand that you are forgiven in your head but have difficulty absorbing this thought in your heart, then perhaps it is time to open yourself up to showing more love to other people yourself. In time, your heart will soften.

Sometimes we have trouble accepting the love of God, or even the love of those around us, not simply because we feel guilty over past actions, but also because, deep inside, we feel that we are intrinsically unlovable. If this feeling is strong enough, we may even hate ourselves for having whatever attributes that we think makes us so unlovable. When we don't feel loveable, then as we interact with the world around us, we anticipate pain and

Accept God's Grace

rejection and this anticipation leads us to build walls of
isolation–isolation that prevents us from getting hurt by
others. This isolation, though, also prevents us from
feeling loved by others.

Usually this feeling of being unlovable is rooted in
some artificial yardstick of worth. We may feel unattrac-
tive–perhaps too short, too tall, too wide or too thin. We
may feel we have too much acne, not enough hair, the
wrong sized nose or the wrong colored skin. We may feel
unathletic–unable to catch a ball or shoot a basket. We
may feel poor–unable to afford good clothes or buy a
friend a meal. We may feel too smart or not smart enough.
We may feel socially awkward–unable to carry on a conversation without feeling foolish. Sometimes these yardsticks are thrust upon us by parents, friends, or neighbors
who have struggled with life themselves; sometimes we
create these yardsticks on our own, out of desperation, in
an attempt to make sense of an unkind world.

The funny thing is, if you take the time to get to know
people from different walks of life, you will realize that
those that feel they are loveable don't feel that way because
they measure up to a yardstick, they feel that way because
they don't have a yardstick–they have a creator. Genesis
1:26 describes this creation: *God said, "Let us make man in
our image, after our likeness ..."* and Genesis 1:31 continues:
*And God saw everything that he had made, and behold, it was very
good.* This *everything* includes you. Anyone who looks upon a
newborn baby understands about the baby what God
understands about us: that we are inherently wonderful.
Our value doesn't come from the yardsticks of the world,
our value comes solely from the fact that we are made in
the image of God.

Letting go of the yardsticks that have made us feel rejected can be difficult. We may be able to feel compassion
for others who struggle with their own yardsticks but then
aren't willing to show that same sense of compassion for
ourselves. If you are holding onto one of these yardsticks,

20

then you may need to admit that you are hurting and in pain and then have enough compassion for yourself to allow yourself to let go of the yardstick and rest in the hands of Christ.

Just as there are artificial yardsticks that we hold onto that make us feel unworthy, there are also artificial yardsticks that we hold onto that make us feel superior. These yardsticks lead us to feelings of pride and keep us from accepting God's love as well. Our need to feel accepted can cause us to hold fast to whatever it is that makes us feel so important. Our pride, then, drives us to focus our lives around our yardstick of success, suppressing all other aspects of life. If our yardstick is beauty, then we become vain, if our yardstick is a profession, then we become workaholics, if our yardstick is money, then we become gluttons. In the process of our "success", we drive others away because we have centered our life on our own achievements rather than on God, and we consciously or unconsciously force our yardsticks on those around us. Prideful yardsticks have an additional danger. As the ancient Greek philosopher, Heraclitus, noted, *The only thing that is constant is change*. When we allow the foundation of our life to hinge on money, looks, athletic ability, or any other such yardstick, then our life suddenly loses all meaning if something changes and we lose it.

We cannot fully experience God's grace as long as we hold onto these worldly yardsticks. Letting go of the yardsticks and allowing the walls of isolation and pride to come down, leaves us vulnerable to more pain. However, it also leaves us vulnerable, perhaps for the first time, to real love. It is an act of true faith to let your walls go, but when you do, when you turn to God and finally say *Lord this is who I am*, then God will reach down and wrap his arms around you, just as Jesus described so clearly in the parable of the prodigal son: *his father saw him and felt compassion, and ran and embraced him and kissed him* (Luke 15:20).

PRAY

Every year, as the fall college semester prepares to get underway, young couples are separated as one or the other leaves home for school. Imagine a young man, as he prepares to climb into his car, telling his girlfriend: *I love you so much, I'll text you every day*. Sounds romantic right? But then imagine that he tells his girlfriend that he has half a dozen messages pre-programmed into his phone. This one says *I love you*, this one says *I'm thinking of you*, and this one says *I miss you so much*. Continuing on, he says: *I promise to send one or two of these to you every day*. How thrilled would the young girl be? Probably not overflowing with excitement, at least not the type of excitement the (possibly ex-) boyfriend was hoping for.

Relationships grow deeper through intimacy, through self-revelation. The young girl wants to know how her boyfriend is doing *today*, how he is *feeling*, what he's excited about, what he's depressed about. She wants to be part of his life. The same is true of God. God wants to be included in your life.

When the Bible talks about prayer, it is talking about building intimacy with God. Unfortunately, prayer, for many of us, can become little more than sending prepro-grammed text message. How many of us have learned how to speed through a *Bless us, Oh Lord, and these thy gifts which we are about to receive from thy bounty* prayer before the com-mercial break is over? In Matthew 6:7 Jesus says that *when you pray, do not heap up empty phrases as the Gentiles do, for they think that they will be heard for their many words*. He then continues on to say *pray like this* and prays the prayer that is now known as *The Lord's Prayer*. The sad truth is that, when we rotely recite the Lord's prayer, we are doing exactly what Jesus told us not to do. He didn't say pray *this* prayer, he said pray *like* this. Reciting a well-known prayer or singing a hymn with family and friends has value because it builds and re-enforces a sense of community, but it is not a substitute for true prayer.

Understanding that Jesus cares primarily about our hearts, we can discern what he was trying to teach us in this passage by looking at the attitude of his prayer. The prayer opens up with *Our Father in heaven, hallowed be your name*. The fact that Jesus started with the word *our* rather than *my* shows that Jesus recognizes that he is part of a community and that the guy he thinks of as his special father is also the special father of the others as well. Jesus is also professing his recognition of and appreciation of the fact that God's character is hallowed, meaning that it is set apart from all sin, perfect in love, and full of mercy and grace. Often when friends meet or get together, especially with men, there can be a little competitiveness to the conversation. This can come out in subtle ways—through a strong handshake or a slight up-tilt of the chin. When coming to God, though, there is no room for this silliness, just love. The attitude Jesus is projecting is the attitude of saying *Hey, Dad, you know you are so wonderful I am just so thankful that I have this opportunity to talk to you.*

You ever had a good friend come up to you and tell you how you should run your life? I've had well-meaning friends try to convince me to get a babysitter so I could go on vacation somewhere for a week. They didn't think I was balancing my life right and thought they knew all the answers. What they didn't understand was that, for me, being with my kids *is* a vacation. They didn't understand the goals and values I have for myself and my family. In the same way, we do not have a full understanding of God's plans for us or the rest of his kingdom. When we go to God in prayer, telling him everything that he should be doing (*Lord, please give me a sports car.*), one can imagine him sitting back, smiling, and just shaking his head a little. Rather than telling God what to do, Jesus prayed *Your kingdom come, your will be done, on earth as it is in heaven*. We want to be close to God because we love knowing that he accepts us, we appreciate the mercy he gives us, and we want to experience more of the feelings of joy and happiness that he has promised us. It only makes sense, then, that our prayer should be that he continue to do things his way in the world. In fact, the sooner the better.

We tend to have many expectations of ourselves, of others, and of God and, when things do not align according to our expectations, we get stressed. The American Institute of Stress estimated that stress costs the American economy over $300 billion dollars annually. Anger and depression are the result of stress, and both cause not only economic loss but also damage friendships, often hurting those who care about us the most. For many, the stress resulting from frustration has led to substance abuse, anger, depression, or detachment–all of which destroy families and relationships in tragic ways. Why then, do we expect that things will always go right? Why do we expect that, tomorrow, the things that we have today will still be with us? This is not what God promised us. We never expect to lose a loved one and, when it happens, the grief can be overwhelming, but how often do we fail to appreciate the blessings that we have *today*? If God has graced us with a husband, a wife, or children today, why do we snap at them when we should be enjoying the blessings while we have them? Solomon, in Ecclesiastes 3:4, reminds us that there is *a time to weep, and a time to laugh.* We need to stop worrying about the inevitable times of weeping and learn to fully and uninhibitedly enjoy the abundant times of laughing. We need to stop holding on to the unrealistic expectations that bind us with fear and anxiety over the potential loss of that which we are failing to enjoy today.

What we should expect in this fallen world is for all those around us to struggle, with varying degrees of success, with their own selfish desires, with jealousy, with anger, with depression, and with self-righteousness. We should also expect times of sickness and death, uncertain economic times, challenges at work, and challenges at home. We should expect these things in the same way that we expect the rain. We cannot always know when it will come, but it will come. All of these things are components of this experience known as life and, rather than be stressed that it is happening to us, we should learn to appreciate the abundance of it. In Luke 12:25, Jesus asked *which of you by being anxious can add a single hour to his span of life?* The time spent wringing our hands over our frustrations could also be spent appreciating those things that God has provided us today.

I was reminded of this a few years ago at the death of my father-in-law. He had wished to be buried in his hometown, several hours north, and we found ourselves relying on extended family to organize the service in that small town. As difficult and sad as the funeral was, I could not help being overwhelmed by the love and kindness exhibited not only by our extended family, but also by the church community in that small town that pulled together to prepare food for the service. Losing a loved one is one of the most frustrating experiences in life because we can do nothing about it. During this time, my sense of frustration was eased when I allowed myself to experience God's abundant love poured out on us through our family and that small community. God answered my confused prayers of anguish by providing a loving extended family and church community, which he had prepared in advance, to meet the needs of hurting people like me. How often are we so consumed by our stress that we overlook and ignore our answered prayer when God has been gracious enough to give us what we need rather than what we may have asked for?

If we focus on the uncertainties of life, then out of this errant focus will bloom anxieties, and these anxieties will soon control our lives. However, in the next line of the Lord's prayer, Jesus teaches us simply to ask the Father to *Give us this day our daily bread.* Jesus is helping us to focus on the present, trusting that God will provide for us what we need today.

What is interesting, again, is how Jesus concludes the request for our daily bread with a request for God to *forgive us our debts, as we also have forgiven our debtors.* Jesus is reminding us that God *knows* that we will have debtors, people in our lives who will have hurt us physically or emotionally, but he encourages us to join in God's spirit of forgiveness. Jesus conveyed the importance of this more boldly in his parable of the unmerciful servant (Matthew 18:21-35): *"You wicked servant! I forgave you all that debt because you pleaded with me. And should not you have had mercy on your fellow servant, as I had mercy on you?" And in anger his master delivered him to the jailers, until he should pay all his debt. So also my heavenly Father will do to every one of you, if you do not forgive your brother from your heart.*

If we learn to live our lives with this attitude of trusting God rather than worrying about the future, fully appreciating what each day brings, appreciating every transgression inflicted upon us and viewing them as exciting opportunities to extend compassionate grace to those who afflict us, then our lives will be filled with peace. Jesus knew, though, that we may have, just occasionally, days that don't work out so smoothly; days in which we stumble. It is these days that our spirits are at risk because, when we stumble, we tend to reach for shortcuts. Days we are low on money, we may be tempted to steal; days we are frustrated, we may be tempted to lash out at friends; days we are hurt, we may be tempted to hurt others; and days we feel no love, we may be tempted to withhold forgiveness. We need to accept that we are broken, that try as we might, on our own, our failures will be more than occasional and we need to ask God to be there on these days, to be our shield against these things that always end up bringing us more pain and pulling us further away from God. This is the attitude Jesus is conveying in the concluding verse of this prayer: *And lead us not into temptation, but deliver us from evil.*

If God had a cellphone, we'd probably come closer to praying at the times we should. Cellphones have enabled us to let friends know where we are going with a quick text message, to share a special moment by sending a photo, and to call and talk when we've got a problem or just need to listen to the voice of a friend. Like any good friend, God wants to be part of your life, he wants to stay in touch, he wants to be able to celebrate with you, comfort you, guide you, and protect you.

Praying to God can, at times, be a challenge—we don't always know what to pray for. The Gospels showed that Christ spent much time in prayer; he regularly retreated to quiet places to spend time with his Father. What we learn from this is that, first and foremost, we need to simply keep God looped in with what is going on in our lives; James, the leader of the early church in Jerusalem made this point when he wrote *Is anyone among you suffering? Let him pray. Is anyone cheerful? Let him sing praise* (James 5:13). The Apostle Paul let us know that we can bring all our problems to the Lord; in Philippians 4:6, he wrote *do not be anxious about anything, but in everything by prayer and supplication with thanksgiving let your requests be made known to God.* It's not surprising to learn that God wants us to share the problems and joys of our days with him; what may be surprising is how evident, in the letters of these early leaders of the church, it is that many of their prayers were focused on others. In Romans 1:9-10, we read *without ceasing I mention you always in my prayers* and, in verse 10:1, *Brothers, my heart's desire and prayer to God for them is that they may be saved.* Jesus, of course, also encouraged us to pray not just for friends for, in Luke 6:28, he tells us *to bless those who curse you, pray for those who abuse you* and again, in Matthew 5:44, he says *love your enemies and pray for those who persecute you.*

If you've ever had a friend come to you only when they needed money, you'll understand that it begins to feel more like emotional blackmail than a relationship, so avoid the trap of thinking of God as a vending machine or personal bank. There is no doubt that God has performed miracles in this world, but demanding miracles isn't what prayer is all about. It is about allowing God to transform your heart. The sad truth is, we miss most of the miracles God works in our lives. Whenever a friend stops by, right when you need one, do you remember to thank God?

As you pray for yourself and others, remember that Christ came to us as a brother, and God shares with us that he is our father; in other words, the Lord is family, so relax, be yourself, and remember that prayer is a casual conversation, not a shopping list.

FORGIVE

On July 4th, 2000, first responders raced to the scene of a capsized boat in the frigid waters of New York Harbor. They went into action the moment they arrived at the scene, pulling a drowning man up and into their Zodiac® rescue boat. It was nighttime and the boaters had been on their way back from watching the 4th of July fireworks. By the spotlight from an overhead helicopter, several other victims could be seen flailing helplessly in the water around them. What would you think of the rescued man if he yelled back out to the remaining victims: *Hey, stop splashing water on me, it's annoying–and keep it down, your shouts are giving me a headache!* The very idea of it sounds appalling, doesn't it? However, isn't this what we are doing when we fail to forgive those who hurt us? God has rescued us from our sins–sins that no doubt hurt others. The people who continue to hurt you physically, emotionally, or spiritually, are like the drowning people in the harbor, splashing cold water at the one who's already been rescued. In their situation, without the Spirit of Jesus in their hearts, they can hardly help but to hurt other people.

While others may injure us through their self-serving actions, the more dangerous and potentially damaging

31

injuries are the spiritual injuries caused from the grudges that we hold against the people whom God calls us to forgive. We need the attitude of God that is willing to release these grudges through forgiveness. So often, rather than having this attitude of forgiveness, we hold an attitude of vindictiveness—we want those people to *pay* for what they have done to us. The truth is, people who continue to hurt others, who continue to sin, pay a price every day because they live without the love of God, without a sense of true purpose, without any sense that they are acceptable. They frequently try to escape this void through thrill seeking, violence, drugs, money, and empty relationships. Other than compounding the trail of pain inflicted on others, each of these evasions does little more than create a white noise in their consciences, a buzz just loud enough to cover the steady moaning of their souls. So just as we want God to free us from our past sins, so we should also forgive those who sin against us.

For those who have hurt us badly, even though we come to realize that we should forgive and that failing to forgive is only hurting us, it can still be difficult. If we find ourselves in this situation, then it is necessary to think about *why* we don't want to let go. Sometimes it is because we feel strongly that those who hurt us be held accountable for what they've done. It is not wrong to think this way; in fact, God demands accountability. Romans 14:12 tells us that *each of us will give an account of himself to God*. The key point here is that God reserves the responsibility of this judgment for himself. This is emphasized again in James 4:12: *There is only one lawgiver and judge* [God], *he who is able to save and to destroy. But who are you to judge your neighbor?* God reserves this right for himself as a means of blessing you. It is a burden to attempt to judge the souls of those who hurt you, and God does not intend for you to shoulder this particular burden.

Understand that while we are to forgive, rather than judge our persecutors, our forgiveness does not mean that we condone what they have done nor does it mean that we need to allow them to hurt us again. Forgiving them means that we release them from any feelings of resentment, revenge, or desire for justice—in other words, we no longer hold the sin against them. While Christ teaches that we must forgive even those who continually and unrepentantly sin against us, he cautioned his disciples in Matthew 10:23: *When they persecute you in one town, flee to the next.* God did not create us to be punching bags—we need to protect ourselves from those who do us harm. Forgiving someone for breaking into our house doesn't mean that we shouldn't get a better lock for our door.

The deepest hurts we've suffered are usually the ones inflicted on us when we were young, helpless, or alone. Once you accept Jesus and join the fellowship of other believers, you are no longer alone. Christ is with you in Spirit and with you physically through the lives of fellow Christians. With the power of the Holy Spirit and the support of fellow Christians, you can stand up with grace, dignity, and self-control to those who may continue to try to manipulate, belittle, or otherwise abuse you. Titus 1:13-14 conveys instructions the Apostle Paul sent to his friend Titus, who was leading an early church in Crete. Paul had heard that there were people hurting the early churchgoers by trying to manipulate and twist the beliefs of these new Christians and so his instructions were to *rebuke them sharply, that they may be sound in the faith.* In the same way, standing up for yourself and rebuking those who hurt you or others are not actions that are contrary to forgiveness; rather, they are complementary to forgiveness when done in a spirit of love. The first of these actions helps people understand the sins that they are committing, while the second demonstrates the loving Spirit of Christ, who is available to them when they repent.

Many expect that God will protect us from persecutions, but the Bible does not teach this; rather, it teaches Christians how to respond to the persecutions which we will inevitably face. Matthew 5:44 instructs us to *Love your enemies and pray for those who persecute you.* Romans 12:14 tells us to *Bless those who persecute you; bless and do not curse them.* Rebuking is just one way of blessing those who persecute you because the rebuke provides an opportunity for the person to see, from the outside, their own sins.

Holding on to unforgiveness can give us a sense of control over the person who hurt us. We become a jailor, keeping this person in a prison constructed of our own hatred. However, responding to hate, with hate, only serves to increase our own sense of bitterness, just as responding to anger with anger only serves to increase our own emotional numbness; we may think that our hostility gives us control over the other, but it is, in fact, we *ourselves* that become imprisoned by our own destructive attitudes. There is no wisdom in seeking to control another person. If you think about it, God never tried to control us. He's cautioned us, guided us, taught us, confronted us, and admonished us, but he has always given us our freedom. Attempting to keep control over those who hurt you only hurts yourself and only prolongs your own misery.

Prolonging misery, thought, is a reason why some do hold on to unforgiveness. We will relive old arguments and confrontational experiences over and over in our heads and wallow in a spirit of dejectedness so that the person who did this to us will be punished by being forced to watch us suffer. The truth is, however, we may have become so used to the misery that we have gotten comfortable with it. Change is uncomfortable and, surprisingly enough, being happy can be uncomfortable when you are not used to it, but God wants you to change; he wants you to *be transformed by the renewal of your mind.* Learning to forgive is a necessary step in this transformational process. Do not be afraid of the uncomfortableness that you may experience. God knows that this can be hard, which is why he sent us the Holy Spirit, who brings us comfort.

God Worthy?

A final reason we may hold onto unforgiveness, is that we are simply not emotionally ready to confront the hurt. In a letter to the church Paul founded in Corinth, he wrote *... whatever is true, whatever is honorable, whatever is just, whatever is pure, whatever is lovely, whatever is commendable, if there is any excellence, if there is anything worthy of praise, think about these things* (Philippians 4:8-9). When we've been hurt badly, the memories of that hurt can be like a wet blanket over lovely thoughts. If you find that hurtful feelings unexpectedly intrude on even the good moments of your life, you need to make a commitment to confront this past. One of the best ways to confront these past hurts, is to sit with good friends and share your story—many times over, if necessary. Through this sharing, you will learn to accept that you have been hurt, but also accept that the events that caused this hurt are behind you. You may also find that, intermixed into those painful times of the past, were good times—positive experiences had with those involved in the pain that can serve to amplify the hurt when seen as an opportunity lost. Take comfort in these positive experiences, and instead of dwelling on what might have been, accept both the good and the bad as part of the story of your life, and let them go. Every day adds a new page to this story, and as we learn to accept and acknowledge the pain of the past, we can also learn to accept and acknowledge that some measure of joy awaits us in our future chapters—and this joy has the right to be experienced unfettered.

With this renewed spirit, accepting that the lives of those that hurt us are, themselves, a jumble, we can finally release them to forgiveness—even if we, ourselves, are the perpetrator of our own harms.

Letting go of past hurts, forgiving others, forgiving ourselves, and if necessary, forgiving the Lord are all honorable, commendable, excellence things, worthy of praise. Think on these.

LOSE THE RULES

When I was very young, a rule was instituted in our house: we may not paint the walls with excrement taken from our diapers. A year or two later, we had an additional rule: we may not decorate the walls and furniture with paint taken from daddy's oil-painting kit. When I was in kindergarten, an additional rule was issued: we may not write our names on closet doors with mommy's fingernail polish.

As a child, the idea that my actions may cause anguish, stress, or work for my parents didn't factor into my thinking in any significant way. I tended to live in a more self-centered world and viewed my parents as caretakers, rule givers, and disciplinarians.

Something happened, though, as I transitioned through my teenage years into young adulthood. My view of my parents changed. I began to see them as loving people who had done their best to raise me and look after me. As I've grown older still, I now enjoy spending time talking and sharing with them as people, and you know what? When I go to their homes to visit them, there are no rules. I do not write on their walls with anything, I do not track mud onto their kitchen floors, and I do not drink directly out of their milk cartons, but I don't refrain from doing these things because there are rules against them; I refrain from doing these things because I care about my parents.

As we grow from children to adults, our relationship changes from one based on rules to one based on principles. For some, this is a difficult transition. In many ways, living by rules is easier: you always know where you stand (or at least you think you do) and, therefore, you can continue to live in a self-focused world. Living by principle, in contrast, requires thought and discernment. You need to think about how your words, actions, or inactions may affect or influence other people's lives, emotions, and self-image—even in the smallest of circumstances. For example, when you go out to dinner with a friend, societal rules may dictate that you split the check, but you need to ask yourself: which will show more love, following this custom, picking up the check yourself as a gift to them, or allowing them the pleasure of giving to you?

When people live by principles, they look to do what is right; when they live by rules, they look to do what they can get away with; rules are made to be broken, principles are made to be lived. A company that I worked for had a receptionist who began showing up for work in provocative clothing. Many corporations, for better or worse, operate with a rule-based mentality so, when confronted with this problem, the company issued a new policy: no skirts may be worn shorter than knee length. The following week, the receptionist arrived at work in a knee length, skin tight, leather skirt with a low-cut blouse. Another policy was issued and the receptionist arrived sporting a plaid skirt and a new blouse that was buttoned up to her neck but was also nearly transparent. There is something about rules that cause us to seek the loopholes, to find ways around them. In some instances, the very existence of a rule generates, within us, a desire to break it. Rules not only encourage a self-centered view of the world, they also encourage judgmentalism. When we live by rules, then it's easy for us to find fault with others because their faults are black and white. They either obeyed the rule or they didn't. We then feel free to persecute that person, which we do, because when their lives are miserable ours seem better by comparison.

Of course, the other thing that we can do when we live by rules is to recognize how frequently we fall short of them, which we then use to beat ourselves into bitterness, numbness, depression, or some combination of these three.

Just as our relationships with our parents change over time, our relationship with God changes when we make a decision to accept and put our faith in Jesus. Galatians 3:24 explains that *the law was our guardian until Christ came, in order that we might be justified by faith.* Once we put our trust in God, he no longer wants us to live in the self-centered world of the law, but rather in the principle-based Kingdom of God, the primary principle of which is to live and act in love.

As 1 Timothy 1:9 tells us, *the law is not laid down for the just but for the lawless and disobedient.* We are no longer to live in obedience to the law, but rather we are to live in obedience to our faith (Romans 1:12). Does this mean that, as faithful followers of Christ, we no longer have to obey the commands of the Bible? Experience shows us that when obedience doesn't come from the knowledge of the heart, the expression of that obedience often doesn't result in a manifestation of love. A friend of mine was chastising a relative who was planning on getting a tattoo, and his lack of support was hurting their relationship. He had recently read Leviticus 19:28, *You shall not make any cuts on your body for the dead or tattoo yourselves: I am the LORD.* Rather than taking the time to understand how God intended this scripture to be an act of love, he took the view that he was trusting God. If God wrote the rule, then it must be love. A deeper study of this particular scripture reveals that, at that time in history, tattooing was done as a sign of worship to other gods. The point of this particular scripture passage is that God desires us to love him wholeheartedly and has nothing to do with whether or not someone wants to tattoo a rose on their ankle. Deep, God-inspired wisdom recorded in the Scriptures can help us understand and discern what true love is, and it is to this love that we must be obedient.

In his book *Escape From Freedom*, sociologist Eric Fromm shares the idea that people will struggle *for* freedom then, when they find it, they struggle *with* freedom. They don't really know what to do with freedom once they get it, and they find new controls and structures to control them. Romans 8:2 tells us that, in Christ, we have been set free from the law of sin and death. It is a glorious moment when we first come to understand that our sins have been paid for and we no longer face that penalty of death for our sins—that we have been set free. Every Christian needs to be aware, however, that our desire to remain accepted and loved by God and by others can drive us back towards easily definable criteria by which we can evaluate ourselves and others—our needs can drive us back to the very rules that bound us to our sins. Many religions cater to this desire for structure, telling us you must do these seven things to be right with God, or you must go to church every Sunday to be right with God, or you must not walk more than 1/2 mile from your city on the Sabbath, and the list goes on. It is impossible to succumb to a religion's rules without giving up the freedom we have in Christ. How can we be free to follow the leading of the Holy Spirit if we have bound ourselves to the constraints of some religion's rules?

Rules make us comfortable because we believe that we always know what we should do and what we shouldn't. However, this comfort leads us to complacency while true faith drives us to learn, to study, and to grow in new ways as we seek to better love the Lord, our families, our friends, and all those around us. The Apostle Paul shared his own experience in growth as he strove to share this understanding with the early church in Corinth. In his first letter to them, he wrote: *For though I am free from all, I have made myself a servant to all, that I might win more of them. To the Jews I became as a Jew, in order to win Jews. To those under the law I became as one under the law (though not being myself under the law) that I might win those under the law. To those outside the law I became as one outside the law (not being outside the law of God but under the law of Christ) that I might win those outside the law. To the weak I became weak, that I might win the weak. I have become all things to all people, that by all means I might save some.* Paul lost the rules and learned to live by faith.

It is interesting that in the very same letter that Paul writes that he is *free from all*, he appears to create a new set of rules with passages such as verse 11:7 where he writes: *For a man ought not to cover his head …* . Paul resolves this apparent contradiction in verse 10:23 by explaining that *"All things are lawful," but not all things are helpful. "All things are lawful," but not all things build up.* Within the culture and customs at the time, men who wore head coverings at church were obviously causing discord with their fellow believers. Paul is not creating new laws for us to follow; rather, he is showing us that, when we live in Christ, our desire will be to find ways to eliminate discord so that others may come to understand God's love, even if it means sacrificing our own freedoms. It's not about the head covering; it's about the relationships.

Our willingness to sacrifice our selfish desires in order to show love for others is a powerful witness to friends or family because they will see, through our actions, that following Christ is ultimately about living a life in love. Blindly following "Bible rules," without seeking to insure that our words and actions are expressing love can, in fact, drive people away from Christ because our example is essentially telling them: *unless you follow this rule, you cannot be a Christian.* If you were to tell your friends that you don't wear a hat because the Bible tells you that wearing hats is wrong, do you think your friends would be more likely to seek Christ? I doubt it. However, if you were to tell a friend that you stopped wearing your hat to church because some new members were distracted by it and you wanted to make sure that they felt welcomed in the church, then this is an example that means something.

Jesus, as recorded in Mark 3:1-6, was confronted by the church leaders who tested him to see if he met their standards—to see if he would follow the laws of the religion or break the laws by healing a man's hand on the Sabbath day. As Mark wrote, Jesus *looked around at them with anger, grieved at their hardness of heart, and said to the man, "Stretch out your hand." he stretched it out, and his hand was restored.* His grief and anger were due to the fact that they had exchanged true faith for rules. As followers of Christ, we must all learn to rely on our faith and lose the rules.

BE KIND TO YOUR MIND

A group of NIH researchers who specialized in adolescent psychology came up with plan, during a hallway conversation, to save millions of taxpayer dollars. They proposed that rather than issue funding grants for expensive research that utilize MRI technology, blind studies, and expansive surveys, they would instead purchase a rocking chair. They would then invite grandmothers to sit in the rocking chair and then ask them questions. For example, they might ask: *Suppose that a young boy lived and played in a neighborhood and, in this neighborhood, there were a number of other kids that used and sold drugs. Do you think the young boy would eventually start using drugs?* The grandmother might pause for a moment or two, and then give them an answer: *Yes, the boy would likely get caught up in drugs.*

The researchers, of course, were joking with each other when they proposed the idea of *granny testing* and, instead, along with other governments and organizations, have invested millions of dollars in research that has concluded that we are tremendously influenced by those around us, by what we watch on TV, and by what we read.

This influence appears in many different ways. Alan

43

Greenspan, former head of the U.S. Federal Reserve Board, studied happiness and found that people's happiness didn't correlate with their wealth, but rather correlated with their wealth as compared to the wealth of those with whom they associate. That is, someone making $50,000 a year who lives in a neighborhood where most people make $40,000 a year are happier than people who make a million dollars a year and live in a neighborhood where their friends make a billion dollars a year. Putting it another way, the wealth of those we associate with establishes a subconscious internal baseline of wealth by which we evaluate our financial success.

Ethics researchers studying corporations such as Enron and WorldCom found that, within those companies, an environment of loose ethics existed and, because of this, employees began to feel that cutting corners and cheating customers was the normal way to conduct business. The same type of problems exist in college dorms and city basketball courts. When we're in those environments and find that most of our friends occasionally shoplift, bully others, have casual sex, or cheat on exams, we tend to believe that this is OK, just a normal part of life. In fact, it is not uncommon for these friends to begin to make us believe there is something wrong with us if we don't do these things as well. Their attitudes subconsciously set an internal baseline of morality by which we evaluate our own moral inclinations.

Using our peers as a baseline for our morality and happiness is not what God intends for us. The Bible teaches us that God himself provides our baseline. The book of Leviticus shares with us that God emphasized multiple times: *you shall be holy, for I the LORD your God am holy.* The word *holy* means sacred or set apart from sin. This is the true standard for which we will be held accountable. Jesus reiterated this in Matthew 5:8 when he said *Blessed are the pure in heart, for they shall see God.* The fact that we tend to adopt the standards set by our peers is just another reflection of the gap that has grown between us and God–a gap that must be bridged.

As we seek to become more like Christ and seek to *be transformed by the renewal of [our] mind[s]*, we need to realize that it will take active participation on our part. It is unlikely that lustful thoughts will leave our minds if we continue to view pornography, and it is unlikely that peaceful thoughts will fill our minds if we continue to maintain close friendships with people who perpetually focus on hatred, anger, prejudice, or selfishness.

Unfortunately, in this world, it is not possible to avoid all the people and media that negatively influence our thoughts. The secret is to continuously dilute the negative influences in our lives with positive influences.

This is why it is so important to develop a small group of Christian friends who will encourage us, uplift us, and remind us of the love of God. In Romans, the Apostle Paul exhorts us to *Love one another with brotherly affection* and *Live in harmony with one another*, and talks of our being *full of goodness, filled with all knowledge and able to instruct one another*. In 1 Corinthians, he says we *comfort one another*, and in Galatians he tells us to *bear one another's burdens*. It is obvious that we cannot do these things if we are not sharing life together and building close relationships with each other. How can someone help us bear our burdens if we keep a wall around our soul? In Matthew 18:20, Jesus tells us: *For where two or three are gathered in my name, there am I among them*. And when Jesus sent the disciples out, he sent them out in twos (Mark 6:7). Jesus does not say and do these things by accident; he knows that life is hard and that staying close to him is hard, so he encourages us to live life together because he knows that these relationships will help shape our hearts. Nowhere in the Bible is there a reference to people baptizing themselves; even Jesus was baptized by someone else. The reason is that God designed us to be interdependent. When we spend time with others who don't share Christ's values, it is difficult to keep our thoughts from slipping back into their old negative patterns.

Although we may recognize the need to shape our environment, the idea that we should give up on our current friendships can be unappealing. Understand that God does not ask us to detach from this world and in fact he left us with the responsibility to reach out to all those who do not yet know his love and share it with them (see Matthew 28:16-20), and we have no one better to start sharing with than our current friends. On the other hand, it is important to consider the depth and foundation of these existing friendships when deciding if they should be preserved or let go. Sometimes we choose friends who will help us validate our own bad behavior. For example, if we drink too much, it is possible that we have attracted friends who also drink too much. If we choose to straighten our lives out and stop drinking, we may find that these *friendships* evaporate rather quickly. We may also come to realize that some of our friendships don't go much farther than a shared interest in sports or a loose camaraderie founded on complaints about the boss or the customers that get in the way of us doing our jobs. The valuable friendships, the one's worth keeping, are those in which a friend will give us a call, if they don't see us for a while, just to make sure we are doing OK. These are the kind of friends who will be excited for us, as we decide to move forward in our spiritual life. They may or may not choose to follow Christ with us, but this kind of friend will appreciate the increased depth of the love that we show them as we grow in Christ.

Is it wrong to maintain those casual friendships, the ones with little depth? Is it wrong to eat candy? Candy is good in moderation, but if we use it as a substitute for food, our health will quickly decline. In the same way, casual friendships are light and easy, not requiring much work, but they don't provide much food for our souls and won't contribute to our spiritual growth.

God Worthy?

In all of our relationships, it is a good practice to monitor the words that are exchanged. Do they tend to be encouraging or discouraging? Do they tend to be judgmental, fault finding, or abusive either to us or others we may know? Do the conversations reflect an appreciation for the unique beauty and value which is inherent in all of God's children, or do they objectivize people? Do they reflect a sense of self-responsibility for one's actions and situations, or do they tend to blame others for these things? If we take the time to think about it, we will realize that our thought patterns and feelings after a conversation are reflective of the tone and attitude of that conversation. If we participate in too many conversations that have a negative tone, it will be hard to keep from drifting away from the fullness of Christ's love.

Personal friendships and relationships are perhaps the most powerful influence on our thoughts and attitudes, but we should be cognizant of others. Growing up, my brother and I spent many hours watching TV, and Hanna and Barbera's *Tom and Jerry* cartoons were always a favorite. I received a call from my brother a few years ago because he, for the first time, introduced his two son's (ages 4 and 3) to the cartoon. At one point, the mouse, Jerry, pounded Tom with a hammer. As the scene ended, my brother saw his older son turn to his little brother, ball up his fist, and pound him on the head. My brother's comment was *maybe TV* does *influence our behavior!*

In the early days of television, most shows went overboard to show lifestyles based on positive values and frequently showed family and friends supporting one another. The content producers today appear to be primarily motivated by greed and are, therefore, more than happy to present ever-increasing violence, treachery, and every manner of twisted morality. Many in the entertainment industry, having gained wealth faster than wisdom, have not realized the need for God and therefore have not come to know his heart and his ways. Much of what we see on television may be a reflection of the untethered values of these producers and writers.

Psychologists have found that imagined experiences can have nearly the same influence as actual experiences in terms of their impact on the mind. This is why it is important to think carefully about media that you choose to watch and listen to. It *does* affect your attitudes and thought patterns and, in particular, it is a large factor in setting the internal moral baseline mentioned above. As an example, years of watching television shows that depict casual sex can ingrain the idea into your head that nothing is wrong with this type of relationship and that it is *normal.* Because of the detached nature of the media, you aren't exposed to the long-term emotional scarring that can come from these behaviors. You don't experience the sense of loneliness and unfulfillment or the long-term damage to future relationships that frequently is the result of these behaviors. You only experience that short term sense of thrill that the shows' producers wants you to experience.

Therefore, it is wise to put similar filters on your media experiences that you put on your friendships. As you listen to music or watch videos, ask yourself how the content compares or relates to the loving nature of God. If your media choices consistently fail in this comparison, then it is likely that they are having a subtle, but negative, influence on your character and spiritual life. On the other hand, we don't need to boycott entertainment altogether. Rockin' out to some favorite old tunes is just fun to do sometimes and so is watching a great movie. The healthy thing to do, though, is to simply check the balance. Are you continuously feeding enough positive things into your head to balance out the negative? Are you being kind to your mind?

READ FOR YOURSELF

Of all the media sources available, plain old books contain the most transformational power for the heart and mind. Reading, for some, can be a difficult habit to develop, but it is worth the effort. The value comes not only from the content but also from the quiet time we set aside to do the reading. Several hundred years ago, people's lives were filled with quiet time in which they could think–in which they could ponder new ideas and evaluate them against their own pre-existing notions of the world. In today's electronic age, this is a rare luxury–our minds have been warped into information-processing machines, absorbing or discarding information in real time. Book reading time can be an exception to this, if we allow it to be. When seeking to understand the heart of God, we have no better book to spend time reading than the Bible.

Of course in the years immediately following Jesus crucifixion, people couldn't read Jesus words, because no one had written them down yet. Instead, huddled in quiet homes, friends, family, and strangers crowded around the Apostles as they told stories of what they heard and saw as they followed Jesus through his ministry. Undoubtedly, these disciples repeated the same stories over and over again to each new set of ears. It's easy to speculate that the retelling of the stories helped the Apostles process all they had learned, helping them to understand and then share with their listeners how Jesus' life was the culmination of all that was written in the early Jewish Scriptures. Eventually, several of these men committed their oft-told stories to paper, providing us the first four books of the New Testament.

For some of us, our assessment of Christianity is primarily influenced by what we think we remember of what people told us about it years ago. Something is lost, though, when our understanding of faith comes through other's explanations. Of course it's always valuable to supplement your understanding of God by reading or listening to people who've thought deeply about their faith, but neither an exposition nor a distillation of the collection of books known as the Bible has the ability to convey the homey, authentic, simplicity of the words shared by the original authors. Pushing aside any preconceived notions of God and reading the Bible for yourself is the best way to feel the truth of his message. By inspiring the disciples to put their stories to paper, and inspiring countless others to carefully preserve those word through the generations, God has enabled us to be among the curious in the room where the stories are being told.

Reading the Bible is both enjoyable and fulfilling if you follow the simple advice given by many pastors. First, and most importantly, find a translation of the Bible that is readable for you. Most translations have study editions available. The advantage of study additions is that they contain footnotes, cross-references, and concordances that are a great aid in understanding more difficult passages and those that take on new meaning once the historical context of the writer is known. Second, rather than be overwhelmed by the Bible as a whole, read one book at a time and, third, do not be discouraged at passages that you don't understand. Most students of the Bible find that passages become clear, and sometimes take on whole new dimensions of meaning, as they grow, over the years, in both spiritual and natural maturity.

There are no hard and fast rules when it comes to reading the Bible, but it does help to understand its structure. As mentioned above, the New Testament opens with the four Gospels (see the sidebar) and, if you are new to the faith, one of the Gospels is the best place to begin reading. Gaining insight on the historical context of the remaining letters of the New Testament is useful background information, so Acts of the Apostles is a great book to read after the Gospels. Following Acts of the Apostles, the New Testament includes a collection of letters written by the Apostles and early disciples to the young churches that were beginning to grow in the years following Jesus' resurrection. These letters are particularly relevant to us today because they address needs that we continue to have. In these letters, the Apostles share the true heart of Christ and give guidance and encouragement to the followers as they struggle to overcome their sinful desires and tendencies.

Until you read the Old Testament, you cannot fully appreciate the depth of God's plan for redemption. The New Testament tells us how Jesus fulfilled the Mosaic Law and prophecies of the Scriptures. The Old Testament is the collection of books that document this law and these prophecies. The first five books of the Bible, known as the *Pentateuch*, were penned by Moses himself and provide a foundational knowledge of the Scriptures. The history of the Israelite nation is documented in the next set of books. Following that, are several books known as the *Books of Wisdom*, or simply *The Writings*. The books of the major and minor prophets follow The Writings. The words of the prophets can be a challenge to understand at first perusal; however, growth in faith and knowledge of the other parts of the Bible generally add clarity to the prophetic books. The last book of the New Testament, Reve-

The Gospels

Each of the four Gospel writers took a different approach to their story. John Mark was a young boy when Jesus was preaching, and evidence suggests that he hung out with the Apostles at times and must have watched with fascination at the doings of Christ. The Gospel of Mark, thought to be the first Gospel written, is very action oriented, telling the readers what Jesus did without as much explanation as the other writers. Matthew, also known as Levi, was a tax collector when Jesus called him to be a disciple. Matthew's Gospel was targeted towards the Jews of the time and shows, in more depth than Mark, how Jesus' ministry served to fulfill the early Scriptures. Luke was a physician and historian who came to know Christ after the crucifixion. He spent significant time in ministry with the Apostles in the days of the early church. His Gospel shares many of the same stories as those of Mark and Matthew; however, his target audience was the Gentiles (Romans and other non-Jews within the Roman Empire). Luke also authored the Acts of the Apostles as a continuation of the historical narrative started in his Gospel. John outlived the other Apostles and, because of that, had a unique perspective on the workings and movement of the Holy Spirit through the early church. John's Gospel is more spiritual than the others and emphasizes the holiness of Christ. Those familiar with the Old Testament will see that John's Gospel sheds illumination on the feasts established by God through Moses as a foreshadowing of Jesus' death and resurrection.

lation, is also prophetic and reminiscent of Isaiah.

With the help of concordances (word indexes located in the back of many study Bibles) and online search tools, additional insight can be gained with focused reading exercises. Looking up and reading all the passages centered around one word or one topic is useful, as is reading all the passages related to a specific individual mentioned in the narratives. Regardless of how you choose to organize your reading, it is always valuable to take time to ponder the words you've read and pray to the Lord that he open your eyes to what the scriptures might mean in your life today. Be prepared for some wrestling in this prayer cycle. Most of us may admit that our first inclination, after reading *Give to the one who begs from you, and do not refuse the one who would borrow from you.* (Matthew 5:42) is tell God "Nope. Not gonna do it." This is a not-uncommon way to open up a prayer dialogue with the Lord. If you continue to ponder and pray on this verse, you may find the Lord opening your eyes to the plight of those in need in your community. At the same time, you'll find yourself rationalizing excuses for avoiding such generosity. This back and forth is the very reason why it is so worthwhile to read the Bible–the process shapes our heart, and so as you are debating with the Lord, think about how you want your heart to be shaped in the process, and trust that the words of scripture speak wisdom.

In searching out the wisdom of the passage mentioned above, you may find that the Lord is leading you not to give cash to beggars on the street, looking to fund their next fix, but to donate food to a food bank, or money to an organization that supports those in need in a constructive way. Read, ponder, pray honestly, trust, and listen. It is how the wisdom of God assimilates into our own consciences, and it is a process that has brought understanding and peace to the lives of Christians for centuries.

Read For Yourself

In order to gain the fullest value from reading the Bible, it is important to understand that these books were written by real people, living in specific times and places that had their own unique (and often quite different from our own) social, political, and cultural landscapes. The words chosen by any author are a response to their own times and are unavoidably targeted towards the mindset and perspective of those living within their own world. For example, when Moses wrote: *God made two great lights–the greater light to govern the day and the lesser light to govern the night* (Genesis 1:16) the Israelites of his day, having been steeped in the culture of ancient Egypt, would have immediately recognized the intentionality of Moses' diminishment of Egypt's sun god, Ra, (the preeminent god of the Egyptians) when he referred to him as a *light*, rather than by his proper name. Moses' purpose in writing this story was to define an identity for the Israelite nation that was separate from that of the surrounding cultures and to ground that identity in their relationship with a single, and superior god: the God of Abraham, Isaac, and Jacob.

To the readers of the time, the correspondence and contrast between Moses' teaching and the prevailing theological ideas would have been abundantly clear, but when we read them, our tendency is to interpret them from our own worldview, one that has been significantly shaped by universally mandated science classes and our ability to fact-check information, instantly, with the entirety of human knowledge being at our fingertips. Our minds are used to the idea of peer-reviewed textbooks, but in ancient times, the only means available to a person to fact check an idea or notion was to leverage either their own memories or the memories of friends or relatives that they knew personally. Because of our resources, today's authors strive for historical and scientific accuracy–concepts that would not have been understood thousands of years ago. In contrast, during the time these early scriptures were written, an author's primary goal was to convey a theme, and so for this reason, when reading and studying the Bible, the value of the text is best absorbed by seeking to understand what that theme was.

While the primary themes of the Bible narratives are discernable without much knowledge of the historical context surrounding the stories, taking the time to understand the nature of the culture of the times can provide a more nuanced understanding of the themes conveyed in a particular writing. Taking the time to contemplate the value, and even necessity, for a society to *have* a communally understood culture helps set the stage for gaining further insights into the workings of God through the progression of time, as seen in the pages of the scriptures.

What we call *culture* is an agreed upon set of standards for social interaction that enable groups of humans to work together for their mutually beneficial well-being. Humans cannot live alone and either because of this, or for this, our brains have been thoroughly wired to live socially. Furthermore, we have been wired to desire stability in our understanding of the norms of social interaction, and this need for stability has both positive and negative consequence.

As a simple example, in American culture most believe that it is polite to call (or text) a friend before showing up at their home for a visit, while in some small towns in rural China, neighbors freely walk into each other's homes at will. Imagine how uncomfortable (or scary) life might be to an American, if a neighbor suddenly showed up in their living room, or how insulted a rural Chinese person might be, if a neighbor sought to formally schedule a visit. So having this common understanding of cultural propriety helps keep the peace. On the other hand, this need for social stability has been part of human existence from the beginning, and because of this, because it is wired into the core of our brains, people have what could be called a neural constraint to the rate of culture change: we automatically, implicitly, and sometimes without realizing what we are doing, resist attempts to change our culture, even when it should be clear that the change could be beneficial

Of course every culture evolves over time, changing little-by-little with every generation. My great-father would likely be horrified by the idea that I dated my wife without a chaperone before we were married. Today, the idea of a chaperone isn't understood. But when change comes too rapidly, societies react, as the clashes of the civil rights movements can attest. New ideas, like equal rights for people regardless of race, religion, or culture, take decades, or even centuries to work their way through a large society without causing widespread strife and bloodshed.

And God knows this.

A stumbling block for many, as they begin to read the Bible, is that God can appear cruel, coldhearted, or insensitive to us living in the more empathetic 21st century. For example, 1 Corinthians 14:34 tells us that *women should keep silent in the churches*, a line of scripture that many today find both offensive and nonsensical. How could a loving God cause women to be treated so shabbily? The answer lies in understanding the neural constraint to the rate of cultural change. Within the culture of the times, it was commonly understood that women would not speak up in churches and instead talk with their father or husband when they wanted to discuss the scriptures. If God had inspired his disciples to give women the right the vote and encourage them to run for political office, it would have caused chaos in the streets and the resultant backlash would counter-act all that the disciples had shared. A careful reading of the Gospels reveals that Jesus respected women immensely and even revealed himself as the messiah for the first time to a women (see John 4). The apostle Paul, who penned 1 Corinthians, also had great respect for women and included them in his ministry. But God was not interested in causing chaos and social unrest. He is a God of peace. Scripture passages that we see today as cruel and coldhearted, in fact reveal a God that is patiently, and slowly, working within the cultural norms of each successive generation to progress a message of untiring grace, compassion, and love. Having said that, I'd rather live today, than be a Philistine in king David's time (see the books of Samuel and Kings).

It helps, when trying to understand why God may appear insensitive, or even cruel, to recognize that there is a direct line of inspiration from the early scriptures to the advent of hospitals and orphanages, to the right of women to vote and for the right of African Americans to choose what neighborhood they live in. 1 Samuel 27:9 tells us that when *David attacked an area, he did not leave a man or woman alive, but took sheep and cattle, donkeys and camels, and clothes.* If God stopped David in his battles and raids instead of ignoring the common cultural practices of warfare of the day, then David would have never written *The Lord is gracious and merciful, slow to anger and abounding in steadfast love* (see Psalm 145) or any of his other Psalms, and the hearts of countless generations would not have been warmed by them.

Without the patient work of the Lord, incrementally shaping our collective hearts throughout the millennia, our hospitals and orphanages, and many of the rights we enjoy today would not exist.

David did not see the cruelty in his actions and neither did the businessmen who put *Whites Only* signs in their storefronts only a few decades go. A question for each of us to keep in the forefront of our minds is to wonder what cultural norms we currently accept that may be holding us back from a more complete acceptance of the underlying theme of God's love. Similarly, we can ask ourselves: How can we learn from the Lord's example to have patience with people who hold tight to old cultural standards that hinder societies adoption of what we might consider a more righteous state of being? And finally, the reverse of that: How can we have empathy for those who are suffering from the loss of stability and sense of identity caused by the rapid changes in our society that *are* taking place.

If we allow them, the Holy Scriptures can lead to a new perspective of life, and our approach to it, through the wisdom we garner from our contemplation of the themes conveyed in the individual books and also by stepping back to perceive the patiently consistent and loving way our God has worked to heal our brokenness across the span of scriptural history.

LOSE FEAR–GAIN UNDERSTANDING

A few years ago, I was transferred to a different division within the company I worked for and found myself reporting to one of those nightmare bosses. Everything I did was wrong and everything he did was perfect. Occasionally he'd call me into his office to rip into something I'd done–wanting to know why I did something this way, why I failed to do it that way, and so forth.

After working in the office for a couple of weeks, the other employees began to share their opinions of the boss with me. It seemed that everyone hated this guy, and they would seize upon any little thing he did as an opportunity to tear him down behind his back as a means of retaliation and vengeance. At first, my anger at being treated so unfairly caused me to get sucked into the gossip chain like the rest of them but, eventually, I began to come to my senses. I knew that joining in on this kind of gossip was not the loving thing to do–it was not following the example that Christ had set for us. After some time, I began to notice something else about the boss that the others

59

seemed to have overlooked. He had no friends. He ate alone, he worked alone, and he left alone. In fact, as far as I could tell, the only time he actually spent conversing with someone else from the office was when he was issuing orders or complaining about someone.

Witnessing all this made me recall something I had read in Les Giblin's book, *How to Have Confidence and Power in Dealing with People*. In it, he equated people's egos with hungry dogs. Just as a dog will get downright nasty if it isn't fed, so will a person get downright nasty if their ego isn't fed. Les goes on to explain that when a person doesn't receive any outside encouragement, they will begin to feed their own ego. This book taught me that retaliating against a nasty person who is "full of themself," only makes the situation worse–you are simply continuing the starvation. Because I had read the book, I knew how to handle the situation. As I continued to work with my boss, I began to seek every opportunity to compliment him on his ideas and his successes. It was tough going at first because he didn't quite know what to make of it. After a while, though, I began to see a shift, and soon our conversations became quite cordial. If I had never read that book, I would have never understood how to relate to someone like this.

This wasn't the first lesson I learned from a book. As a young adult, I never felt comfortable at parties. I had a number of occasions when I'd be invited to one by a friend but, when I arrived, I found that I didn't know anyone else in the room. It is one of the most isolating feelings in the world to be in a room where everyone else has grouped themselves into close-knit conversation circles and you know that you aren't part of any of their cliques. Reading Don Gabor's *How To Start A Conversation And Make Friends* was, for me, like opening the door to a whole new world. The book was simple enough but provided me with an understanding of interpersonal dynamics that I had never really understood before, helping to teach me how to feel comfortable and get to know new people in these situations.

Some people think that *people skills* are a God-given gift, but they aren't a gift; they are a skill, and skills are something that you learn. Some, through circumstances in childhood, acquire these skills at an early age. They can step into any circle of folks at a party and instantly feel like part of the group: this is rare. For most of us, meeting new people, and especially developing the courage and skill to build meaningful relationships, seems quite unnatural and uncomfortable. If you've read through the New Testament, though, you will find that avoiding discomfort is not part of the Christian program. Discomfort is simply the feeling we have as our spirits grow. It is a sign of change and, as a Christian, we learn that a feeling of discomfort usually means that we are on the right track. In terms of relationships with others being *unnatural*, that isn't an idea coming from God's perspective. Having meaningful relationships with others is exactly how God intended our natures to be. It is our fear and apprehension that is unnatural. Not all quality books on general people skills, marriage, or parenting are Biblically centered; however, they can help us understand ourselves and why we are the way we are and why others are the way they are as well. As we come to understand people better, the quality of our relationships will deepen, and the fear and anxiety associated with new relationships eases.

As the Apostle Paul found out, learning people skills is invaluable when we begin to have the desire to share the love and message of Christ with others. In Acts 9:23-25, we learn that Paul had to run for his life after preaching about Christ for the first time; then later in Acts 14:19, we find that the town of Lystra stoned him after he preached. Paul was a brilliant scholar and spiritually on fire, but he had not yet learned the people skills necessary to effectively share the gospel. He was not dissuaded, though, and we can discern from the letters he wrote later in life that he had become a master at working with and encouraging others. On several occasions, we learn of people traveling for days just for a chance to visit Paul. For those of us without this natural ability, it is worthwhile to take the time and effort to build these skills.

Most of what we know of the Apostle Paul, we know from the thirteen letters he wrote that comprise a good portion of the New Testament. A reading of Dale Carnegie's *How to Win Friends & Influence People* provides a very interesting perspective on Paul's letters–it appears that Paul mastered many of the same techniques that Dale Carnegie describes in his book as he encouraged the early believers to shed their fears and live with a loving and courageous spirit.

When selecting and reading books that are intended to help you grow, you must use good judgment and discernment. There are numerous books based on pop psychology and many more that describe ways to manipulate people, both of which will have an effect on your personal growth opposite to that intended. Friends, pastors, or pastors who are friends are great resources for book recommendations.

WATCH YOUR DIALOGUE

Our friends, the music and videos we watch, and the books we read, all serve to shape our minds and determine our views of the world and ourselves. Our own voice is an additional, powerful molder of our minds. We build ourselves up and we tear ourselves down by what we say to ourselves in the quiet of our own thoughts, and therefore, just as we must learn to be aware of and monitor the other influences on our minds, we must be aware of and monitor the internal dialogue that we have with ourselves. We must be particularly wary of several distinct types of dialogues.

Dialogues in which we assign attributes to ourselves define who we are. Human beings have a natural tendency to live up to, or down to, the attributes that have been assigned to them. This is why Paul frequently assigned positive attributes to the recipients of his letters with opening verses such as this one in his letter to the Romans, *I thank my God through Jesus Christ for all of you, because your faith is proclaimed in all the world*, which he then followed with sixteen chapters chastising them for all the things wrong with their life in faith. Whenever we say to ourselves things such as *I'm not good with people, I'm not a compassionate person,* or *I can't pray well*, we are further ingraining these weaknesses into our minds. Each time we catch words like these in our heads, we need to learn to stop and replace them with thoughts such as: *I haven't acted as compassionately as I should have in the past, but I'm going to focus on this and work to grow a little more compassionate each day*. It is always useful to do self-evaluations to identify areas of strength and weakness, but when we choose to self-assign weaknesses as inherent attributes, we are doing little more than making excuses to ourselves as to why we should not put forth the effort to improve in those skill areas.

Anyone who has raised a young child understands that the ability to make excuses for ourselves develops early in life. Parents put a great deal of effort into breaking this pattern in our children but we, as adults, don't always put enough effort into breaking the pattern for ourselves. When we hear a child exclaim *I'll never be good enough*, or *I can't do this*, we know that they just need a little encouragement and perhaps a bit of help. When we hear ourselves say it, we take it as fact and then use this fact as an excuse to give up on growth. No one likes to fail. Making excuses is nothing more than a technique that we use to evade a task or goal, of which the path to success has become obscured. A wiser course of action, when we begin to hear the sound of excuse in our voice, would be to reach out to a friend or pastor and ask for help. Children have an intuitive understanding of this and never hesitate to ask for help; over time, though, our pride builds and serves as a stumbling block to the transparent sharing of our weaknesses with a Christian friend and thereby dooms us to stagnation in Spiritual growth. It is for this reason, that James reminded us of the Scriptures, telling us that *God opposes the proud, but gives grace to the humble* (James 4:6).

Two types of internal dialogues that are particularly harmful to our sense of compassion (the subject of a future chapter) are those in which we insult or demean others and those in which we are critical of other's choices, especially when we choose to mentally replay these critical thoughts over and over until our emotions overflow with resentment and anger.

How often do we find ourselves thinking thoughts such as *who taught you how to drive? My blind dog could merge better than you!*, or *they are such idiots, how hard is it to do this and so?* Why is it that we allow ourselves such unkind thoughts? When someone is having difficulty, why don't we instead remind ourselves that we've had days when we have struggled as well; that we've found ourselves in situations that are a little over our heads. Wouldn't it also be prudent to take a moment to thank the Lord for providing you with the strength, the IQ, the driving skill, the friends, the money, or whatever it is that is making you feel so superior to this other person?

Critical thoughts act as a slow poison to our relationship with God and our relationships with others, as do thoughts that demean others, particularly those that, in our own minds, reduce others to objects of our lustful thinking. When we think to ourselves *oh!, look at that smokin' hot body*, we are deliberately overlooking the fact that this person is a beautiful child of God, one that wants to be valued and appreciated for who they are as a person. God created us with these bodies, and he's the one who wired us for physical attraction as well, but this design was intended to support committed marital relationships where physical attraction is only one component of a love and appreciation for one another that goes far deeper. Allowing ourselves to dwell on lustful thoughts of others when we are married is particularly harmful because these thoughts demean the object of the lust, they subtly damage the appreciation we have of our own spouse, and they tear away at our spouses feelings of trust and relational security. People should never feel guilty about the thoughts that spontaneously pop into their heads; however, if we want to continue to grow to be more like Christ, we need to learn to treat them like a bad television rerun: changing the channel as soon as they appear on our mental screens.

Dwelling on the choices of others whom we have found to be disagreeable has, surprisingly, taken its toll on many Christians who otherwise appear to be quite mature in their faith. Ask any pastor or any church music director, and they will likely tell you they've experienced this first-hand, either as culprit or as victim. We forget that each and every one of us shows up in the world a little bit broken, with our own custom-tailored set of inadequacies, and we have to make our way through this world the best that we can. The only way to avoid making bad decisions and wrong choices is to make no decisions or choices; the truth is, taking this route is the worst choice of all. If you have a family, a job, or a church, sooner or later, your life is going to be affected by the bad choices other individuals make. It's amazing how, in a loving family, if a brother or sister makes a questionable choice, the family will stick by them, support them, and be there for them to help make things work out, but if a co-worker or pastor makes a bad choice, then it's *Game On!*

The thoughts and emotions usually spiral out of control when we have our own clear vision of how something should be. This could be anything from the way to properly load a truck, to the type of music that is played in worship, to the arrangement of dishes in the kitchen cabinet. When someone with authority or influence makes a final decision that thwarts our vision, then we get frustrated; our own choices in the handling of this frustration can lead us either into turmoil or into grace. When we make the love of God a priority in our lives, then we begin to search out ways to bless those responsible for and affected by the decision. Most skilled craftsmen understand that an important part of their craft is always being ready to adapt to mistakes. A wood carver who digs too deeply with his lathe chisel will suddenly adapt a design that called for one large ridge into a design with two smaller ridges; adapting to mistakes is just part of his craft. It can be difficult to sacrifice our own vision of music or kitchen-cabinet arrangement but, when we make the sacrifice, we do it as an act of selfless love to someone who may need more examples of selfless love in their lives. On the other hand, when we choose to refuse any sacrifice, then we leave our internal dialogue to spin unchecked. The decision does not go away and neither does our dissatisfaction with it; feelings of helplessness give way to feelings of resentment and feelings of resentment give way to feelings of anger and, finally, the feelings of anger will give way to either hatred, separation, or both. In either case, the relationship is lost.

Nowhere in the Bible does it suggest that we should limit our relationships to only those individuals who make perfect decisions. A careful reading of the New Testament letters encourages Christians to learn to support one another in spite of the inevitable decisions that come out of our broken natures. As the Christian faith first began to spread in Rome and as non-Jews began taking on leadership roles in the churches of that city, great conflicts emerged over decisions on whether or not it was right to follow Jewish dietary laws. The type of frustration, resentment and anger discussed above began to brew, threatening the relationships and fellowships that underlie the very foundations of God's kingdom. Paul, a man who sacrificed everything to help others understand the peace of God, lovingly wrote to these churches: *Therefore let us not pass judgment on one another any longer, but rather decide never to put a stumbling block or hindrance in the way of a brother. I know and am persuaded in the Lord Jesus that nothing is unclean in itself, but it is unclean for anyone who thinks it unclean. For if your brother is grieved by what you eat, you are no longer walking in love. By what you eat, do not destroy the one for whom Christ died* (Romans 14:13-15).

Jesus encouraged his followers to serve in unity as he made this offer: *if two of you agree on earth about anything they ask, it will be done for them by my Father in heaven. For where two or three are gathered in my name, there am I among them* (Matthew

18:19-20). All too often, Christians find that they need Jesus among them, when two or three are gathered, because they need a referee. Jesus didn't promise that God will be with us when we make good decisions; he promised that God will be with us when we support each other and work together and, as Romans 8:31 tells us, *if God is for us, who can be against us?*

Jesus' encouragement to work in unity should not be taken as a license to bully other Christians, nor should it be taken as a command to be bullied. The idea he was conveying is that it is more important to maintain harmony than to be right and more important to maintain cooperation than to insist on our rights. We can trust that God will work good works through our hands, regardless of the quality of our decisions, if we work together with love and unity.

Therefore, ask yourself the next time you catch angry resentful thoughts cycling through your consciousness, *Am I feeding my head thoughts that are in line with my priorities, in line with my growing closer to God, in line with my understanding his heart? Or am I choosing to instead scar my mind with a dialogue of stubbornness?*

CULTIVATE HUMILITY

In the opening of this book. I mentioned that God doesn't want to change who we are. But truthfully, that was an ambiguous assertion.

What does "who we are" mean? Physically, we are the same person on the day we die as we were on the day we were born, but when we think about who we are, we are actually thinking about how we define ourselves.

Many default to answering this question of who they are in terms of their occupation: "I'm a truck driver", "I'm a teacher", "I'm an auto mechanic". Others will define themselves in terms of their general demeanor: "I'm a friendly person", or "I'm an angry person", and still others would answer this question in terms of their real or perceived status in society: "I'm a victim", "I'm an outcast", "I'm a hoodlum", or "I'm a winner".

Psychologists have put thought into this question of how we define ourselves and have come to use the term *identity* to describe the notion. Our *identity*, they will tell you, is derived from our worldview, from the sum total of all the things in this world that we believe to be true.

And because of this, it is a valuable exercise to dig

deeper into understanding how we form the beliefs that we hold.

Some time ago, I attended a men's retreat where a man spoke about his life experiences and how each new idea learned from these experiences was like a card added to the card-house of his life. Each new card, or each new lesson, built upon the foundation of the others. One problem, he shared, was that humans have an amazing ability to "read between the lines"–inferring new information from previously held facts, and that we end up incorporating this inferred information into our card houses as validated facts, even though our inferences tend to be over-simplifications if not outright wrong.

By way of explanation, he shared that when he was young, his father left his mother and the family. As a young child, his brain added a new card to his card house that told him that marriages end in pain and divorce. Other experiences, including sexual abuse and having the family move to a rougher neighborhood, added additional cards to his card house of life, and so by the time he was an adult, he had a large and complex card house. In his early twenties, he met and fell in love with a young women and soon she was ready to get married. The problem though, as he explained it, was that the idea that he could be loveable, and that this love would last, was like a card that didn't fit in his card house. In order to force-fit it in place, other parts of his card-house would necessarily collapse, and due to some internal force that he couldn't explain, he wasn't willing to let that happen. He wasn't willing to allow his card house, his sense of identity, to change.

Why is it so difficult for us to allow our beliefs to be altered? Again, over the past half century, psychologists have developed a body of research to help us understand this. They have observed that people have a number of biases, or "mental shortcuts" that we use when processing new information. One of the more widely documented biases has been termed the *confirmation bias*. What this describes is the fact that most of us will readily accept any new thought or idea that confirms a previously held belief and casually dismiss any other new thought or idea that contradicts a pre-held belief. In other words, if you've always thought of yourself as someone that is ugly or unlikeable, and some new acquaintance makes friendly overtures to you, reaching out for conversation or even an invite to a lunch, you are more likely to dismiss this as someone being polite than to accept the idea that some new person is interested in getting to know you better. On the other hand, if someone directs a demeaning remark your way, you are likely to accept it and the pain that comes along with it, if it fits the pre-existing ideas of who you are. Confirmation bias impacts all areas of our life, from our notion of our own personal attributes, to our political views, to our views on what constitutes proper behavior at a social gathering.

Another shortcut we make in our thinking is something called the *Dunning-Kruger* affect. This is widely studied phenomena were its been found that people tend to have high confidence in their abilities in tasks or fields of knowledge for which they have no real training or ability. Our ignorance of the complexities of a person or subject gives us great confidence in our own reductions. For me, this is most easily seen at a sports bar, as countless fans discuss how they could manage a professional ball team better than the coach of the team they are watching. The danger in this, of course, is that it prevents us from learning and growing. While we may be itching for a chance to give this coach a good piece of our mind, because of the Dunning-Kruger affect, an actual professional ball coach, whose training frees him from this affect, would probably welcome an opportunity to talk to this coach after a losing game, to hear about his challenges and to understand why he made the decisions he made, with the thought of learning something new.

Cultivate Humility

In addition to minimizing our ability to learn, Dunning-Kruger shapes our relationships with others in a damaging way, because it discourages us from actively listening to them with care or treating their thoughts and ideas with the seriousness that they deserve. This hurts those we are interacting with, because it sends the unspoken message that their views are unvalued and unappreciated.

A third bias that psychologists discuss is one termed *cognitive dissonance*. When we learn how to overcome the Dunning-Kruger affect, willing to accept that we may have gaps in our understanding, and then overcome our confirmation biases, so that we do not readily dismiss a differing idea, then we can still fall victim to cognitive dissonance, which is the phenomena of believing two contradictory ideas at the same time. For example, after reading the Bible, we may come to have faith in the idea that Jesus died for all our sins and to believe that we are welcomed into the Kingdom of God. But at the same time, in a corner of our brain, a voice is still telling us that we don't belong. Two contradictory beliefs that have plagued Christians throughout time.

Because of our propensity to infer information that isn't there and our brain's continuous use of these mental "shortcuts", it is imperative that we all come to recognize that each of us goes through life with some measure of error in our beliefs. We all have a perspective that is not quite in line with that of the Lords.

So how do we work around these biases so that we can begin to see the world as it really is, as God sees it? By cultivating an attitude of humility.

Prior to Jesus' crucifixion, an attitude of humility was seen as a weakness. Strength, confidence, and arrogance were the attributes valued in the ancient civilizations. From the opening story of Jesus birth, as told in Luke chapter 2, we see that Christ was born to peasants and his birth was announced to shepherds, the lowest of the lowly classes at the time. He was born in a barn in an animal trough, the epitome of ignoble. He circulated among the poor and working class, and being crucified like a common criminal was a final demeaning blow to his reputation. The gospels emphasized this aspect of Jesus' life to help us understand that many of the ideas and concepts that we hold to be true, that we use to define ourselves and assure ourselves that we have value, are considered meaningless from God's point of view. In 1 Peter 3:8, Peter wrote ... *all of you, have unity of mind, sympathy, brotherly love, a tender heart, and a humble mind.* These are the attributes and components of our identity that God values for us, each of which, serving to support the others.

Paul recorded similar sentiment, encouraging the early believers in the city of Philippi to *Do nothing from selfish ambition or conceit, but in humility count others more significant than yourselves* (Philippians, 2:3).

While it is important to be humble towards one another, often this is made easier if we first humble ourselves before the Lord, because, as King David record in his Psalm 25, *He [God] leads the humble in what is right, and teaches the humble his way.*

Most of us have learned to thrive or at least survive in this world by leaning on our own understanding–by using all the hard life lessons and experiences that we have accrued to guide us into the future. So accepting the exhortations in the scriptures to humble ourselves to the Lord is difficult to put in practice, because it means letting go of that bubble of protection that is our own worldview. But is it too hard to think that our all-knowing and all loving god may know something that we don't? That he may know new ways to bring happiness to the lives of ourselves and our families? Each one of us has lived on this earth for only the shortest breath of time; therefore, it is reasonable to assume that the ideas of the god who created the Earth and that has been watching over humanity for all the generations, may not immediately fit within our own understanding. And this assumption, in turn, implies that we should not feel so comfortable dismissing the promptings of the Lord. When deciding what to do after encountering a new teaching from the Lord or a prompting of the Spirit, it may be worthwhile to first ask ourselves what is the risk? Is life lived in our own bubble of protection so perfect that it is not worth exposing ourselves to the wisdom of God?

Kathryn Schulz, in her book *Being Wrong: Adventures in the Margin of Error* brings to light the fact that having flaws in the ideas that define our sense of identity is inherent in human nature and goes on to describe how challenging it is to let go of these ideas. Because of this, we can get stuck in life, holding onto notions of ourselves that no longer have to be true. We may have grown so comfortable with the idea of being the angry person, or the plumber, or the bigshot that we don't want to see more.

Transformation, though, happens when we humble ourselves to God and to others, and listen.

Sam Tushabe was 25 years old when God caused him take notice of the orphaned children rummaging for food in the trash heaps of his hometown in Uganda. As AIDs swept through the country, the surviving widows found (and still find) themselves overwhelmed as the orphaned children of their friends and relatives began arriving at their doorstep. But with limited income, there is only so much food to go around. If you asked Sam Tushabe, at the time, if he could launch and run an international AIDs foundation and a network of schools aimed to meet the needs of orphans and widows in Africa, I'm sure he would have laughed. But one day, a widow who was already struggling to care for eight orphans reached out to him in exasperation, because a ninth had shown up on her doorstep, and with her meager income, she could not afford to feed one more. That was the first orphan Sam Tushabe supported. When he was supporting ten, he knew that he could do no more, and so he began writing to churches, begging for help, and as the help grew, Sam's idea of what he could do grew, and AOETs first orphanage and school was opened. Missionaries from America showed up, one summer, to help with the school, and within the group he found men with backgrounds in finance and experience managing large organizations. Sam could have shared with pride all that he had accomplished, but instead, he humbled himself to these men, who lived in a culture far different from his own and who knew little about the social structure and family values in rural Uganda. He listened and learned from them as much as he could, gaining valuable lessons that would help him grow his ministry further. Today AOET cares for over 4000 orphans, along with widows and others impacted by AIDs and the poverty in Africa because Sam Tushabe humbled himself to the Spirit of the Lord and humbled himself to other men.

With a similar story, Vicki Blackson, in her retirement, volunteered for her first missions trip, and while in Ukraine, the Lord opened her eyes to the plight of children born with disabilities in societies that view birth defects as a curse. Vicki humbled herself to the Lord, and he led her to become co-founder of *Every Child is Worthy Ministries*, which provides support and education for parents of the disabled in remote parts of the world.

It is easy to get comfortable being the angry person, being the plumber, being the hoodlum, or even being the bigshot. It is so comfortable that our brains don't want to let go of our self-conception and see what else God may have in store for us.

Many of us default to defining ourselves by who we used to be, we rarely take time to update these ideas to who we have become, and once we leave childhood, almost never define ourselves in terms of who we *can* become.

It takes humility to overcome the undercurrent of error in our beliefs and to release the pride and arrogance that hold us back from what we can become. That same humility opens the doors to our relationships with others, providing them the sense of purpose and acceptance that they deserve. Listening with humility doesn't mean we need to accept as true everything that people say to us—that wouldn't make sense. But whenever we do listen, we should set a goal for ourselves to be open to learning something new, to finding one new perspective that we can use to enhance our own worldview. But even when we don't agree with an idea that people have shared with us, we at least have come to know that person a little better, and so we can learn to love them, just a little more.

In this way, we cultivate humility. By recognizing our own biases, by being aware that our own views may be flawed, and by being open to learning from others and learning from the Lord.

Through this cultivation, it will become apparent that the fact that we navigate through life with some measure of error implies that others do as well, and just as we need to be accepted in spite of our flaws, fears, and failures, others do as well. In this recognition, born of humility, we grow.

And as we grow, we may find that we too have developed the talents and skills to launch a new ministry. But even better, we may find that we have grown to be a more thoughtful husband, wife, parent or child. A more compassionate boss or more supportive co-worker, a friendlier neighbor and a more generous friend.

Luke, in his gospel account, recorded Jesus' words as he prayed in the Garden of Gethsemane, waiting for the soldiers to arrest and crucify him: *Father, if you are willing, remove this cup from me. Nevertheless, not my will, but yours, be done* (Luke 22:42).

Submission is humility in action and has been an exhortation in the scriptures from the earliest days as something to be offered, not demanded. Submission is the powerful bridge between what we can accomplish alone and what we can accomplish together with God, and with each other. When hearing the word *submission*, many think of Ephesians 5:22, where Paul wrote *Wives, submit to your own husbands*, and some latch on to this as evidence of gender bias, an evil they perceive in the world. How few look to Paul's words directly preceding this sentence encouraging us to submit to one another.

We have all seen people argue over inane things, from the proper way to grill a hamburger, to what company makes the best smartphone, and so it should be obvious that without offering our own submission, little will be accomplished in the world.

When people fail to submit to one another, relationships fail, along with all that could have been accomplished through those relationships. The fallout of this failure frequently includes friends and co-workers parting company, walking out of each other's lives.

While God values all relationships, in our weakness he knows that some may fail, but he has called out marriage as one relationship that should not fail because of the parallels he has drawn between marriage and our relationship with him. For this reason Paul chose to place specific emphasis on submission within the marriage context, which is exactly where many of us find submission to be the most challenging.

What makes submission so difficult is that it relies on trust, which sprouts from humility, and whose shoots grow only when watered with transparency and fed with caring love. Therefore, to grow your love through submission, discipline yourself to take advantage of every opportunity for trust.

Jim a friend of mine, shared a story of one such opportunity early in his marriage:

Some years ago, my wife and I were driving to a friend's house, and I was getting ready to turn left at an upcoming intersection when my wife says, "we need to turn right here". Now we hadn't been to this particular friend's house often, but I was fairly confident that we needed to turn left, and so I had a decision to make. Do I trust in my own judgement, or do I submit to my wife's idea and turn right. Well, I turned right, and after a little while, it became apparent to both of us that we were going in the wrong direction, and so I turned around and went the way I wanted to go in the first place, and arrived a few minutes later than we had planned. But how did my decision impact our lives? By trusting in my wife and submitting to her point of view, I let her know that I valued her and her opinions, and it strengthened our relationship. Over time, the habit of mutual submission and trust has built our marriage into strong relationship, as it does in any relationship.

What is the cost of trust? Well if you are a neurosurgeon getting ready to drill into the left side of your patient's skull, and a nurse intern says "no, drill in the right side", then perhaps that is not the time for submission. But in most circumstances in life, the cost is insignificant when compared to the value infused into the relationship, and quite often, you'll find that when people learn to listen to each other, trust each another, and submit to each other, they get to dinner parties on time more often than not.

DEVELOP COMPASSION

The garden of Eden had no pain. God had created a world that was pure, free of disease, free of disasters, and free of the selfishness that now so entangles our lives. In that world, they did not need mercy and compassion; these are forms of love born out of the pain of this broken world and designed to make our brokenness tolerable.

We all know this pain, we all know loneliness, loss, despair, and fear, and somehow we also know whom to turn to when we can bear it no longer. Expressions such as *there are no atheists in foxholes* and the plaintiff *God help me*, testify to this fact. God wants people to turn towards him in tough times, and he wants us to lean on him, but prayers such as *God help me* are self-centered prayers; they are a response to our own pain. What about a response to other's pain? Are we even aware of their pain? Experience tells us that our instincts for this second category of pain aren't so noble. When we see neighbors, co-workers, or strangers in pain, time and again, our response is to detach, to separate ourselves. Sometimes we do this so that we don't get caught up in their issues. If we are honest with ourselves, though, usually we detach because we just don't want to expend the energy on them, and we console

79

ourselves with the notion that these other people wouldn't want our help anyway. We humans have an amazing ability to compartmentalize our morality.

Jesus understood these tendencies and shared a few parables to help us understand that this attitude is not OK and is not acceptable. In the parable of the good Samaritan (Luke 10:25-37), Jesus tells us that we are to love our neighbor and, by *neighbor*, he means anyone in need. As you read this parable, you'll find that the Samaritan paid a price for his compassion; he paid a price in time, in convenience, in miles walked, and in hard currency. Most of us give money to charity and may even help out in a soup kitchen every once in a while. These are good things, but this isn't what Jesus is driving at. Jesus is calling us to make this personal with the people that we come face to face with on a daily basis, personal with every one of his children who are out in this world, suffering with pain.

Unless you were raised in an abusive home, the type of compassion Jesus is calling for will come naturally to you within your family. When your brothers, sisters, children, or parents are hurting, you reach out and comfort them; and when they hurt you, as happens in every family, you are ready to forgive them. There are two intriguing passages in the Gospel of Matthew, verse 12:50, in which Jesus says *For whoever does the will of my Father in heaven is my brother and sister and mother,* and verse 22:30, *for in the resurrection they neither marry nor are given in marriage, but are like angels in heaven.* Jesus is helping us to understand that in our brokenness, we have created tiered love. That is, we extend one level of love for some people, our immediate family, and a lesser level of love for close friends, and the very lowest level of love for strangers on the street. Godly love, however, has no such tiers. Godly love is perfect and extends to everyone. This can be a hard concept for us to understand, to accept. Part of the reason for our reluctance is that we may hold the notion that our love is a fixed quantity; something that, if we give away too much to one person, will diminish the supply available to another. This is a false notion. The truth is, love tends to multiply; the more we love others, the more love we have to give because, in loving others, we grow closer to God.

Any time we begin to recognize the disconnect between the loving attitude that we *should* have and the loving attitude we *do* have, our response should be to go to prayer. A simple prayer exercise can help build the sense of compassion for others that Jesus was talking about. The exercise is modeled after Jesus' instructions to his disciples when he told them *you will be my witnesses in Jerusalem* [family] *and in all Judea and Samaria* [neighbors/coworkers]*, and to the end of the earth* [everyone else] (Acts 1:8).

Each day, pray for your immediate family and, as you pray, think about their strengths, their weaknesses, their hurts, and their transgressions, and also think about how much you love them, how much you forgive them, and how much you hope that their day will be blessed.

Once you are finished praying for your family, move on to your neighbors, co-workers, or other people who may be your associates and, as before, pray through these same things: their strengths, weaknesses, hurts, and transgressions. Then pray about how much you care about them and how much you forgive them. Take time to think about them individually as human beings, real people dealing with life the best they can, just as those in your immediate family do.

Finally, pray for your enemies—those people at work that make life difficult, neighbors who are inconsiderate, whoever they may be, and pray through these same things. Again, take time to think about these individuals who may be dealing with their own set of issues, perhaps insecurities, fears, loneliness, whatever it might be.

Why include enemies in this prayer list? Because Jesus tells us to. In Matthew 5:44-46, he said: *Love your enemies and pray for those who persecute you, so that you may be sons of your*

Develop Compassion

Father who is in heaven. For he makes his sun rise on the evil and on the good, and sends rain on the just and on the unjust. For if you love those who love you, what reward do you have?

If you have the discipline to pray the prayers outlined above every day, then in a few months, you will notice that you do begin to see people in a new light; you do begin to care and you do begin see with the heart of God.

Several years ago, a new co-worker joined a project team I was on and, in short order, began making enemies. On several occasions, she burst in on me, furious with some decision I had made or action I had taken. Quite frankly, there were a number of times when I never did figure out what she was upset about. As you might expect, people began to avoid this new teammate and, of course, a storm of gossip swirled its way through the organization. I had the same frustrations as everyone else, but I took the time to see something different. I began to think how lonely she must be. Growing up I had a sister who, for the longest time, had the knack of saying just the wrong thing at the wrong time and ended up losing many friends because of it. I remember how hurt my sister was when she found herself alone. I began looking at this co-worker with the same sense of compassion I had for my sister, and I began looking for ways to extend a little friendship and, perhaps, begin to fill the void of loneliness I knew she must feel. Had this girl joined the organization before I knew Christ, I would have closed the door like the rest of the team, but I had come to realize that I had an opportunity to share just a little of what God had given me.

Throughout this process, I was not able to fix the gossip problem, and I was not able to mend all the relationships, but God doesn't call us to fix people; he calls us to love people.

In Luke 6:31, Christ told us *as you wish that others would do to you, do so to them.* In a sense, Christ is telling us to see ourselves in the other person's shoes. In order to do this, we need to take the time to think about what shoes they are wearing. Are these the shoes of someone who grew up in poverty or from a broken home? Are these the shoes of someone who grew up in a rich home, where money was valued and quality time was not? Are these the shoes of someone who never had a teacher who cared enough to reach them, someone who perpetually struggles with feelings of inadequacy? Are these the shoes of someone who has never been appreciated, someone who fills his own ego because no one else ever has? Are these the shoes of someone who has been betrayed, who has lost all sense of trust in relationships? Are these the shoes of someone who has always been a little different, someone who has always been socially awkward, someone who has never had the comfort of feeling like they belong?

How would you feel if you were the one who lived in those shoes day in and day out? How would you feel if your neighbors or co-workers talked behind your back, never truly cared how your day was going or, worse, simply treated you as if you didn't exist? How would you feel if God steered a Christian into your path, but that Christian chose to ignore you as well?

As you develop this habit of praying for people and more sincerely acknowledging them as your spiritual brothers and sisters, it can still be a challenge to actually understand their shoes; that is, understand who they are, the problems they face, or the needs they may have. Techniques are available to us, though, that can help with this challenge, the simplest of which is to engage them in conversations and ask.

For those of us for whom this simple task is unnatural, engaging in such a conversation may seem awkward, so understanding the basic principles behind a dynamic personal conversation can help. Fundamentally, true conversations are based on trust, which is developed through incremental amounts of self-revelation. Generally, conversations open with discussions of facts or events, such as *how about all this rain?* Self-revelation occurs when you make yourself vulnerable by sharing a feeling; *I tend to feel down on gloomy days like this.* One key to maintaining a successfully deepening conversation is to make sure your self-revelations remain incremental. Sharing that *I was committed to a mental health facility on a gloomy day like this* too early in a conversation will send people running for the hills.

Three other ways to get someone to rapidly draw back into their shells is to offer quick solutions to their problems, minimize or dismiss their problems, or pronounce judgment on their actions. Observant husbands will learn this first guideline early in their marriage. We may think we are being helpful, but when we offer solutions to someone else's problems, it is difficult to make the offer without appearing condescending. The very suggestion of our solution implicitly assumes that we did not think that they were smart enough to think of it themselves, and it also suggests that we understand their situation thoroughly enough to know just the right solution for their problems. Most often, people don't want our solution; they simply want someone to lean on as they work out their own solutions. And who, when they are feeling down, needs someone to point out exactly why they are a such a bad human being? Most people know their own weaknesses, or at least know as much as they can handle at the moment, and they don't need you underlining and highlighting them. Once a solid relationship has been established, you will have moments to offer concrete solutions and hold friends accountable. These are important aspects of a Christian relationship, but the first step in compassion is just to listen and allow people the opportunity to fully talk out their own problems. Allowing them to talk is allowing them to clarify, in their own minds, what their feelings, their anxieties, and their desires are. How often do we find someone willing to do this for us?

It may seem obvious, but when seeking to understand another person, it is important that you actually care and are interested in what the other individual is saying. Have you ever been in a conversation when the other person continually turns the talk back around to themselves? *Speaking of paperclips, let me tell you about my last vacation … .* Rather than thinking of what you want to say next, try listening carefully to the other person and look for clues to additional leading questions you could ask that might tell you more about them. For example, I was at the motor vehicle administration the other day with my daughter and asked the woman behind the counter how she liked working at the MVA. *It's one step up from prison*, she replied. It would have been easy to let the conversation end at that point; her response was simple and direct, yet it wasn't. The truth is, most people are desperate for someone else to care about them, to care about their lives, and to care about what they have to say. This woman's answer was analogous to a fisherman casting out a line; she dropped a small clue to her life to see if I would take the bait. I asked the obvious follow-up question (*so you worked in a prison?*) and, as the conversation progressed, I soon learned about a past internship and her hopes and dreams of future career advancement. When engaging in conversation, listen to what other people say not only through their words but also through the expressions on their faces, the way they hold their shoulders, or the way they lean either forward or backward in their chairs. Listen carefully in this way and watch for the bait; it is through the bait they cast that they will lead you toward their very souls.

Compassion isn't about bandaging bleeding wounds; it's about easing each other's pain, and the most pervasive pain in the world is that pain from the feeling that we are on our own, that no one cares. Taking two minutes to acknowledge the people around you, to brighten the day of a tired worker at the MVA, is one of the best exercises in compassion that you can do.

Develop Compassion

On a pleasant spring day in 1991, a beautiful ten year old girl named Rachel was playing in her basement with a friend. Rachel was a lively girl who loved swimming and softball and was frequently seen out in the front yard playing catch with her dad. At 2:30 pm, a shot rang out from the basement: a shot that changed Rachel's life forever. Rachel and her friend had thought that the pistol they found packed away was a toy gun. A helicopter ride to shock-trauma and forty-one hours of surgery prevented the bullet that penetrated her skull from taking Rachel's life, and ten weeks of torturous physical therapy taught her how to walk again. However, the carefree days of running and playing were over. Most kids going through high school agonize over the embarrassment of a bad hairdo or clothes that aren't as fashionable as they should be. At 2:30 pm that day, the entire right side of Rachel's body became partially paralyzed forever. Never again would Rachel be just like the other kids.

Painful and traumatic experiences can be a challenge—their scars can leave us with feelings of anger, depression, and isolation. They can also leave us bitter at the idea of a God that could allow these things to happen and resentful of others whom we perceive as having lives with no such torment. However, these feelings do not need to remain in control of our identity.

Rachel, now in her thirties, was asked: *Do you wish that it never happened?* To which she responded, *No, because otherwise, I wouldn't be who I am.* She went on to explain that she doesn't know what kind of person she might have been if things had been different, but she does know that her trials have transformed her heart in amazing ways; ways which have enabled her see others at a deeper level. *I have learned through my own experience*, Rachel shared, *that there might be a reason people act or behave as they do, and I think understanding that is the first step to compassion. You can't have compassion if you can't see through the outward appearance or someone's mask.* Rachel refuses to believe that this trauma has destroyed her life;

rather, she recognizes that God has wrought, within her, a loving and sensitive heart—a heart that she has used to touch the lives of countless people.

In Luke 16:19-31, Christ tells the story of a carefree man who had no compassion for a pauper named Lazarus and Mark 10:21-22 relates a conversation Jesus had with a man seeking righteousness: *"You lack one thing: go, sell all that you have and give to the poor, and you will have treasure in heaven; and come, follow me." Disheartened by the saying, he went away sorrowful, for he had great possessions.* What was the one thing that the man lacked? Compassion. Compassion, Jesus indicated, is something that does not naturally grow from wealth and comfort, but rather from our own under-standing of hurt and suffering. Hebrews 2:18, describing Jesus himself, says: *Because he himself suffered when he was tempted, he is able to help those who are being tempted.* When we know the sting of hurt and suffering ourselves, we are able to recognize it more clearly in others, and if we allow God to guide our hearts, this recognition drives, within us, a desire to share help and comfort with those in need. As we do this, a surprising thing happens: we end up bringing healing not only to the object of our mercies but to our-selves as well. Philosophers have asked, for centuries, why a god, who is supposed to be good, would allow pain and suffering to exist in the world. No answer to this question will ever satisfy us when we are in anguish. However, we can find, if we allow our hearts to soften, that the pains of this world help us to understand how dependent we are on each other and how dependent we are on God himself. They also allow us to connect, at a deeply emotional level, with those around us who are hurting, and this connection motivates us to push aside our own insecurities and excus-es and offer help.

It is sad how many of us, men in particular, continue in lives without ever making these emotional connections with others out of fear of being perceived as weak or soft. Admitting our human need for love, however, is never a sign of weakness; it is a sign of power and strength. While many may pretend to be intimidating by holding tough expressions on their faces and walls around their hearts, those who we are truly in awe of, are men and women who courageously expose their hearts and are willing to reach out towards others with small gestures and tender mercies. This is how God intends us to live our lives, *[f]or God gave us a spirit not of fear but of power and love and self-control* (2 Timothy 1:7).

Within the agony of pain or the memories of pain, great spiritual gifts lay dormant. Martin Luther King, Jr., born into a society of perpetual racial injustice, could easily have let himself wallow in anger and self-pity for this unfair existence but, instead, he allowed his pain to motivate him to bring about great change for the world. In 1935, Bill Wilson and Bob Smith, both recovering alcoholics, worked together to form a small program to help others consumed by this same disease. Their compassionate effort, known as *Alcoholics Anonymous*, continues to this day. While our society applauds efforts that reach people in the thousands or tens of thousands, the Gospels indicate that God finds it precious when our compassion drives us to respond to even one person. As you read these accounts of Christ's earthly ministry, you will find that the overwhelming majority of miracles Jesus performed provided healing to only a single individual. What Martin Luther King, Jr., Bill Wilson, Bob Smith, and a young girl named Rachel have in common is that they did not allow their painful experiences to bear fruit of revenge, self-pity, isolation, or pride; rather, they leveraged these experiences to kindle a deep compassion for all those around them.

Think of these people the next time you are angry with God and the world, depressed, or even confused over the hard times you've had to endure in life. Learn to notice others around you that may be struggling with pain as intense as your own and then find a way to connect with them. In doing so, you will bring Christ's healing power closer to the both of you.

A friend of mine, an avid football fan, moved from Colorado to Baltimore a number of years ago and enjoys going to the game when his favorite team, the Denver Broncos, are in town. I met him shortly before he went to one such game and found him wearing a custom-tailored coat; the front half displayed the Bronco's colors and logos, while the back half contained the logo and colors of Baltimore's team, the Ravens. He laughingly said that it was to keep him protected from all the Baltimore fans that will be sitting behind him.

Why is it that people can feel great camaraderie with strangers who share a favorite team and feel nothing when hurling insults and an occasional beer bottle at other strangers who support a different team? In a more general sense, we tend to have more acceptance of and more compassion towards people who we can relate to—people who we can understand. This is ultimately the root of all prejudice. Rich people and poor people can look with disdain on one another because they don't take the time to understand or appreciate each other's perspective. The same is true for groups of other religious, ethnic, and cultural backgrounds. Why do we find it so easy to mock the way someone else speaks, dances, or celebrates?

Comfort food is the food that we grew up with, the chicken soup our mother made for us when our throat ached or the bowl of oatmeal we had on chilly winter mornings. Nothing is wrong with enjoying comfort foods but we are missing out in life if we don't diversify our palette, learn to enjoy other cuisines when the opportunities present themselves. The same is true when it comes to people. Most of us feel comfortable when we hang out with people who share the cultural traditions and values we were raised with. Nothing is wrong with cultural and ethnic traditions (most that is), as they provide a great mechanism for maintaining cross-generational relationships and a focal point for shared experiences. As Christians, though, we are called to break away from the attitude of the over-zealous football fan, step back from the comforts of our own traditions, and learn to appreciate people from other backgrounds, as well as people in other stages of life, the way God does. In 1 Samuel 16:7, the prophet helps us understand this view: *the LORD sees not as man sees: man looks on the outward appearance, but the LORD looks on the heart.*

As we strive to see others as God sees them, we learn to appreciate the eccentricities of those around us rather than be repelled by them. In the latter part of the 20th century, sitcoms, as a broadcast genre, grew into a major staple of American television. Million's of viewers enjoyed watching shows such as *Taxi, Barney Miller,* and *Sanford & Sons.* What made the shows so entertaining was the eclectic mix of crazy characters that, over the course of the season, viewers came to love and enjoy. It takes nothing more than a slight mental shift to learn how to enjoy the eclectic mix of people who fill our own lives in the same way we love those characters that we see on TV. Rather than grate your teeth when having to work with people different from yourself, try thanking God for creating a live and in-person situation comedy–just for you. Once you learn to let any resentful or even hostile feelings go, you may be surprised to find how much enjoyment you can get by getting to know how these other people think and, as you open yourselves up to them, you may find that they begin to bless your life in surprising ways. We so often forget that, to them, we are the ones with eccentricities.

Connoisseurs of wine learn to understand and appreciate the subtle flavors of this grape-fermented beverage. They understand the many distinct varieties of wine, from the dry *Pinot Noir*, to the celebratory *Dom Pérignon*, and look forward to every opportunity to sample, savor, and enjoy each of these wines in their own distinct way. As you expand your understanding of the great variety of people brought into your life and expand the sense of compassion you have for them, you will discover that, though you started off seeking to be a blessing for them, they will have blessed you as much or more. You will find that you have become a connoisseur of personalities, appreciating the subtle flavors that they bring into your life.

SHARE YOURSELF

Many pastors have warned that it is not wise to live your life on a theology derived from a single verse in the Bible because of the risk of misinterpretation. The important themes, they will tell you, are restated. Jesus tells us, as recorded in Mark 8:35, *For whoever would save his life will lose it, but whoever loses his life for my sake and the gospel's will save it.* This passage is not repeated in one of the other Gospels; it is, in fact, repeated in each of the four Gospels and twice in both Matthew and Luke.

The essence of this important scripture is that Christ expects us to reach out and serve others as he served us. We have been blessed to know his forgiveness and to know his love, and it is time for us to begin sharing this forgiveness and love with those around us, those who are hurting, those who are bound by the struggles of this world. Jesus passionately preached *You are the light of the world. A city set on a hill cannot be hidden. Nor do people light a lamp and put it under a basket, but on a stand, and it gives light to all in the house. In the same way, let your light shine before others, so that they may see your good works and give glory to your Father who is in heaven* (Matthew 5:14-16).

Share Yourself

Many don't realize that during Jesus' ministry on earth in the few years preceding his crucifixion, he gathered very few followers. Acts 1:15 tells us he had only 120 disciples prior to the arrival of the Holy Spirit. John 6:60-71 confirms that many found it to difficult to accept Christ's teaching. Christ's plan, from the very beginning, was for us to reach out to each other, to share the love of God with others in the same way he shared it with us. Jesus, after his resurrection, made this clear to the Apostles as recorded in Matthew 28:18-20 when he commanded them to *Go therefore and make disciples of all nations, baptizing them in the name of the Father and of the Son and of the Holy Spirit, teaching them to observe all that I have commanded you. And behold, I am with you always, to the end of the age.*

Pretty heavy commandment, isn't it? Sounds like we all have to stand on street corners yelling *Repent! Repent!* Well—not exactly. Christ told us to *make disciples*; he didn't tell us to scare people away, and he didn't tell us to go around pointing out the sins of non-believers. Harping on the sins of non-believers tends to be about as effective as telling a deaf person their piano is out of tune. It won't do anything to improve the tune, but it will get them pretty annoyed at you. In Matthew 10:16, Jesus tells the disciples *Behold, I am sending you out as sheep in the midst of wolves, so be wise as serpents and innocent as doves.* In other words, we are supposed to apply a little intelligence to the task. Two particularly useful preparatory steps are worth taking before setting about doing your part of this commandment to make disciples. First, think back on your own journey and, in particular, what it was that led you to seek a life with Jesus. Take the time to ask your fellow Christian friends the same thing. What you will find in most cases is that someone, or more commonly a succession of people, took the time to get to know you and to model the love of God for you. That's right—we tend to first understand God's love because we see it and feel it from Christians who took the time to care about us. The second useful preparatory step is to read and study the life and ministry of both Jesus and the Apostles and learn from their examples.

In Acts 16:13, Luke records that Paul and his companions *went outside the gate to the riverside, where we supposed there was a place of prayer, and we sat down and spoke to the women who had come together.* Paul didn't find the prayer meeting he was looking for (it was highly unlikely that he and his companions were trolling for women), but it was a group of women that they found who immediately became a group of women worthy of conversation. Paul was a focused evangelist and, upon not finding the men of the town that he had been seeking, could have changed course and searched some other part of the city for the prayer meeting. Paul and his companions, though, were more in tune with the Spirit of God than that. They chose instead to just sit and talk and let this expression of love work its magic. Because of this simple conversation, one of the women, Lydia, accepted the Lord Jesus into her life and ended up supporting Paul and his companions in their ministry as long as they served in the region. Lydia, by some accounts, was the first convert to Christ in Europe.

Love can be expressed in many ways. It can come through a casserole baked for a neighbor who is dealing with one of life's tragedies, it can come from a hospital visit for someone who is lonely, and it can come from a few dollars given to someone who is a bit short at a grocery checkout. In fact, the manner in which love can be expressed is limited only by your imagination. In his classic book, *Try Giving Yourself Away*, David Dunn shares how he will drive past prime parking spaces and park in the back of the lot, just to give someone else the joy of finding a great spot. This is not a meaningless act of kindness, as Luke 8:17 tells us, *nothing is hidden that will not be made manifest, nor is anything secret that will not be known and come to light.*

When players first learn to shoot a ball in the game of soccer, they are taught to plant their non-dominant foot next to the ball, to lock their ankle, to point the toe of their dominant foot in the direction they want the ball to go, and then to kick the ball with their dominant foot, making ball contact with the laces of their shoe. If you've ever watched grammar-school children play soccer, you'll notice that this doesn't go well at first. However, habitual practice, over time, will develop what coaches term muscle memory. The motion will become so natural that the players hardly notice the mechanics of what they are doing.

Kindness, compassion, consideration, caring, and generosity, for Christians, should become as natural as shooting a ball is for a trained athlete. This will only happen if we get in the habit of sharing love. We need to learn to look at each opportunity of human interaction as an opportunity to share love. It becomes easier and more enjoyable each time we do it. David Dunn's passing over of parking spaces may seem silly; after all, does the person behind him even recognize that a kindness has been shown to them? Well, in actuality, acts of kindness do make a difference, for two reasons. First, an act of kindness like this changes the heart of the person initiating it; the act shapes it and molds it to be just a little closer to God's–it builds a little of that muscle memory. Second, the act brightens the day of the recipient. Love doesn't always have to have a goal or underlying motive. Love and kindness are beautiful for their own sake. David Dunn made one day in this broken world just a little brighter for one person. Could you say that of yourself today?

Building the habit of brightening people's day is one of the most productive and enjoyable things a person can do, but it is most especially productive when there is personal contact–an actual human exchange. Inspired by David Dunn, I've made it a habit to try to connect with every invisible person that I meet. Invisible people are the sales clerks, the waiters and waitresses, and others who we typically acknowledge with not much more than rote pleasantries, if we acknowledge their existence at all.

An executive coach I met in ministry shared with me

an exercise that he walks his clients through. He takes them to a shopping mall, picks a person at random, and then asks the executive to tell him twenty things about that person. He's teaching the executives that you can learn much about people by the clothes they choose to wear, the way they've cared for those clothes, the way they take care of themselves, the pace at which they walk and, of course, the expression on their faces. During Jesus' ministry, you find that he always talked to people at their level. When conversing with teachers of the law, he talked as a lawyer; when talking to common people, he talked as a commoner, and so forth. If you read through Acts of the Apostles and the letters that Paul wrote, you will realize that he followed the same pattern. Caring enough about a person to, non-judgmentally, learn a little about them will help you relate in a more effective way. Often, you can find something to complement a person on just from what they are wearing–a nice tie, fancy earrings, or decorative fingernails. A complement is always a winning way to brighten a day. But reading someone's expression can be just as effective. I stopped by a store late one evening and, as I was checking out, I noticed that the clerk had a haggard look on her face, and she was leaning against the back of the checkout stand for support. So I looked at her and brightly exclaimed *it looks like you get really energized by the opportunity to serve so many kind customers!* She just started laughing and then went on to explain that this was her second job, mentioned the bills that had to be paid and went on to share that not all her customers are so kind (imagine). By taking the time to read her body language, I was able to help transform the ending of her day from just another one in a series of drudge, to one ending in a little light laughter. I also gave her an opportunity to share a little of herself in that moment because I was willing to recognize her as child of God, worthy of a few minutes of my attention.

Nudges from the Holy Spirit will be more noticeable to

you as you become willing to open yourself up to others. Christian friends will tell you many stories of times when something *just told them* that they should give a particular old friend a call or walk over and ask a particular person how their day is going and, when they did reach out, they found that the person has just had a tragedy in their life or had reached a low point of depression and was desperately in need of someone to talk to. Christians are God's agents of compassion, and the Lord will guide us to those in need when we become adept at listening to his nudges and ignoring fear's nudges. For whenever we experience that quiet nudge of God, we find that accompanying it is a second nudge of uncertainty born of fear. Sometimes this second nudge is mild, steering us to focus on our busy schedule—telling us that we don't have time to reach out at this moment. Other times, the nudge borders on near panic, with sweating palms and knots of anxiety forming in the pits of our stomachs—as we feel God prompting us to speak to a stranger, an acquaintance, or maybe our boss.

Jesus knows what it is like to experience fear when being prompted to do the will of God. Luke 22:44 describes the night before his betrayal: *being in an agony he prayed more earnestly; and his sweat became like great drops of blood.* Jesus was being asked to go to the cross, but our fear of walking across the room to say *hello* to someone can be just as real. For those who have never been comfortable sharing themselves with others, fear can become almost like a warm blanket, something that we hold onto and use to shield us from God's nudges to live more fully in his kingdom. Like Jesus, though, we need to learn to transfer our trust from this blanket of fear, to our Father in heaven. We need to slowly learn to pattern our life after Jesus.

This habit of brightening the days of sales clerks, over time, will build within you both the heart and skill necessary to reach and relate to other people with whom you have more regular contact, whether at work, the gym, or the classroom. This type of long-term contact provides you with the opportunity of building the type of deeper, more significant relationships discussed in the previous chapter. Occasional compliments and encouragement, coupled with time taken to listen to a person with interest, builds a level of trust that will allow a true friendship to grow. And through this friendship, you will have an opportunity to share, on a more personal level, the reasons behind the faith in God that you hold. What is wonderful about this type of exchange is that God doesn't put the responsibility of converting someone on you. He does ask that you reach out with love, and the Apostle Peter does tell us to *always [be] prepared to make a defense to anyone who asks you for a reason for the hope that is in you; yet do it with gentleness and respect* (1 Peter 3:15). If you are able to help a person come into a relationship with Christ, then you will have found a Christian who is a good friend. If the person does not choose, at that time, to come to Christ, then you will have found a person who may still become a good friend–and nothing is wrong with having a good friend. Who knows? Their time to find Christ may come later.

As we engage in conversations with either strangers or friends, it is always wise to think about what we are saying. When serving at a homeless shelter, letting the conversation drift into how the chef prepared your steak in the restaurant you went to last night might not be kind. When talking with a friend struggling with divorce, then sharing stories about the romantic cruise you just took with your spouse is simply inconsiderate. Conversations are dynamic and it is easy to get caught up in the flow of them, but we need to recognize our tendency to want to talk about ourselves and to talk about whatever thought, experience, or adventure is fresh in our minds but, when dealing with people, we need to remember that *love is patient and kind; love does not envy or boast; it is not arrogant or rude* (1 Corinthians 13:4).

One element of conversation, of which our world is perpetually deficient, is edification and encouragement.

Share Yourself

Think back over your past week. On average, how many words of encouragement did you receive per day? Does this question make you laugh? Did it seem silly to think that you might have received any words of encouragement last week–any at all? Most of us live in a desert of encouragement; when the occasional rain comes, our hearts bloom with gladness like desert lilies but, as in the desert, the raindrops fade quickly, the dry wind comes, and the blooms vanish under the sands of everyday life. As you grow in Christ, as the Holy Spirit fills you with love, train yourself to be a fountain of encouragement and edification for all those around you.

A closing word of caution as you seek to develop these relationships. There is a particular danger for married people who reach out and develop meaningful relationships with people of the opposite sex. *In the resurrection*, Jesus tells us, *they neither marry nor are given in marriage* (Matthew 22:30). Until that time, the risks of jealousy or misplaced feelings are too great to chance in these situations. When someone is in a down point in their marriage (and this does happen from time to time in most marriages) then a warm relationship with someone of the opposite sex has a tendency to shift a person's focus from their partner to the new friend. Marriages can be challenging at times and during these times, it is critical that both husband and wife renew their focus on each other rather than shift their focus to another.

It is uncomfortable and stressful to be in an environment where you don't feel like you belong and this discomfort generates a subtle motivation to conform to those around us. We can find ourselves drinking or partying to excess, we can find ourselves using courser language than is natural for us, and we can find ourselves engaging in conversations that demean and insult others, simply to have the experience of fitting in–without pausing to think that we are creating quite the opposite experience for the targets of these conversations.

As you grow to be more like Christ, you need to become self-aware of this tendency and to recognize when you start saying and doing things simply to fit in. This self-awareness is the first step in fulfilling Paul's advice of Romans 12:2, quoted earlier: *Do not be conformed to this world, but be transformed by the renewal of your mind, that by testing you may discern what is the will of God, what is good and acceptable and perfect.* As you begin the transformation process, you will undoubtedly find yourself in situations or environments where you no longer feel like you belong or no longer feel accepted. You may find that people get upset at you when you don't want to participate in a conversation that will disparage a coworker or you don't want to join the group in a cheating scam or a theft. The Biblical term for this sort of reaction is *persecution*. It may come in the form of simple teasing, or you may find yourself excluded from the group altogether. In some situations and in some countries, Christians have found themselves being beaten or killed simply because they refused to act for any reason except love. Jesus prepared his listeners for this kind of reaction in his Sermon on the Mount with the encouraging words: *Blessed are those who are persecuted for righteousness' sake, for theirs is the kingdom of heaven.* Paul expanded this same thought in his second letter to the Corinthians (2 Corinthians 12:10) *For the sake of Christ, then, I am content with weaknesses, insults, hardships, persecutions, and calamities. For when I am weak, then I am strong.*

Overcoming fears of insults, persecutions, and weaknesses is something that Christians must learn to do. For many, the idea of initiating conversations, as mentioned above, can cause significant anxiety, the root of which is a fear of what people might think of them. A pastor I know used to tell his friends: *if you knew how* infrequently *other people thought of you, you wouldn't worry about* what *they thought of you.* As a Christian, you need to learn to fully accept the love of Christ and, as you do that, acknowledge that God made you the way he made you and that he sees you as a wonderful, beautiful human being who he created to fit into the greater body of Christ. Fear has power only when we choose to discount God's acceptance of us and instead seek the imperfect and malformed acceptance of others. This is hard to do, but know that each time you push aside your fears to extend a tendril of love towards another human being, God is with you and he is delighted in your spirit, as Micah prophesied *[God] delights in steadfast love.* (Micah 7:18)

While your reputation as a Christian may cause people to exclude you from many conversations and outings, your kindness always leaves a mark on people. There may come a time in these people's lives when they need someone they can truly trust, when they need someone to confide in, someone with whom they can share the hurt or pain they are dealing with; at these times, they may seek you out. These situations provide a special opportunity to model the forgiveness of Christ. Rather than turn them away for what they have put you through, you can wipe clear all memories of their persecutions that you have endured and instead extend your arms and ears in friendship. This is sharing yourself as Christ shared himself.

After their weekly games, many athletic teams gather together at a barbecue where they and their families celebrate the week's victories, or console each other over their losses, while feasting on grilled chicken and potato salad. Christians have a similar tradition where we gather together to celebrate our life in Christ and to give comfort to those of us who are facing challenges. We traditionally call this gathering *Sunday Services* or *church.*

This special time of gathering is an important part of sharing your life in Christ because we, as followers of the church, are intended to live and work together as one body and, as Paul relates, *as in one body we have many members, and the members do not all have the same function, so we, though many, are one body in Christ, and individually members one of another* (Romans 12:4-5). In fact, in the Bible, the word *church* doesn't refer to a building or a gathering; it refers to the community of believers.

Would it make sense for someone to show up at a weekly team barbecue but not attend the team practices or games? Of course not. In the same way, Sunday Services should never be considered a check-box, the one hour of the week when you connect with God. Rather it is a time and place where you go to celebrate your weekly growth in Christ, a place to encourage others, and a place to be encouraged. Sunday Services is also a place where your faith can be strengthened through teaching, through the sharing of God's words, and through communal prayer and praise. It is a place to prepare you for the challenges of living a life with Christ in this broken world—not a substitute for it.

While it is important not to go to Sunday Services for the wrong reasons, it is also important not to avoid Sunday Services for the wrong reasons. The last meal that the disciples shared together with Jesus before his arrest, what has come to be known as *The Last Supper*, was the very first Christian "Sunday Service", with Jesus as the pastor. If you read the accounts of this evening, recorded in all four Gospels, you'll find that some of the disciples were arguing over who was the most important (Luke 22:24), one of them argued with their pastor (John 13:8) then "corrected" him (Matthew 26:33), most of them fell asleep when their pastor needed them the most (Matthew 26:40), none of them really understood the sermon that was given, and of course, one of them betrayed their brothers (Mark 14:17).

Church wasn't perfect then and it isn't perfect now, because we have not yet been made perfect. Yet, it was ordained by Christ to fulfill a purpose and that is to enable us to work together to share the love of the gospel message with the world. Within any church body, there will be differences of opinion on the style of governance, the type of music, and the content of the teaching, but the angst of these disagreements can be overcome, just as they were overcome by the first disciples. As Jesus looked around the room that evening, with the echoes of the bickering and pettiness of the past few days still ringing in his ears *Jesus took bread, and after blessing it broke it and gave it to the disciples, and said, "Take, eat; this is my body." And he took a cup, and when he had given thanks he gave it to them, saying, "Drink of it, all of you, for this is my blood of the covenant, which is poured out for many for the forgiveness of sins."* (see Matthew 26:26-29)

These words provide both a calling for the followers to come together, and the wisdom to teach us how to come together in peace by directing our hearts to focus on what is important. Had these first disciples not overcome their differences, you would not be reading these words today—these men and women changed the world. And you have the same opportunity. How did they do it? On a practical level, they met regularly to share the bread and wine, the body and blood, of Christ. They also learned to accept forgiveness from God and from each other, they prayed, they kept their focus on the principles of love, they studied the Scriptures, they taught and encouraged one another, they overcame their fears, they cultivated humility, developed compassion, and they shared themselves with each other and the world. And they did it together, in community.

Just as a car engine is crippled when one cylinder isn't firing, so the church struggles when one brother or sister is missing. It is not possible to live a life in Christ and at the same time separate yourself from fellow believers—the two notions are contrary to each other. Christ intended us to share our lives together through meaningful, transparent relationships.

If you have haven't found fellow believers to share

your life in faith with, then finding a church is a good starting point. The particular worship style or "personality" of the church isn't spiritually important, but there is nothing wrong with attending the church you feel most comfortable in. Regardless of what church you choose to attend, walking in and out of the service with little more than a few handshakes and how-do-you-do's increases the odds of missing the people that could enrich our lives, and also of missing those who might be in need of our friendship. Changing a weekend routine and taking time to engage with new people may seem inconvenient and uncomfortable, but before Christ served that first bread and wine, he knelt down and washed their feet as an example for us. This was certainly inconvenient and uncomfortable, but just as certainly, it strengthened their bonds with him, and with each other.

As you share your love with others each day, and with a dose or two of perseverance, new relationships will grow, the church body will be strengthened, and you'll find that you are closer to, and a contributor to, that promised peace and joy that surpasses all understanding.

CONCLUSION

Imagine that you are a coach of a sports team and that, earlier in the spring, you accepted two new players. The first had amazing talent and was truly a natural at the sport. The second had far less talent but committed himself to be teachable and give it his best. True to his word, this second athlete was the first to arrive at practice every day and struggled, with determination, through every drill. After each practice, he always made it a point to ask you, his coach, for any tips on how he could do better. The first athlete, on the other hand, stopped in for the first practice or two where he performed exceptionally well but then disappeared, never returning to practice again. Now you find that your team has made it to the finals and, just a few minutes before the game is getting ready to start, who walks up to you but this first athlete, announcing brightly: *Hey coach, I'm here–ready to start*. What would you say to this young athlete as the referee is calling you to send in your team? What could you say? The only reasonable answer would be to respond: *I'm sorry–I understand you have talent, but you are not a member of my team.* Even if the athlete pleaded, *I'm really good, I've been practicing on my own every day, please put me in!*, you'd just have to tell him *I'm sorry, but I just don't*

Conclusion

know you.

In this same way, Jesus warned his disciples *Not everyone who says to me, "Lord, Lord" will enter the kingdom of heaven, but the one who does the will of my Father who is in heaven. On that day many will say to me, "Lord, Lord, did we not prophesy in your name, and cast out demons in your name, and do many mighty works in your name?" And then will I declare to them, "I never knew you; depart from me, you workers of lawlessness."* (Matthew 7:31-23)

In government contracting circles, they have a type of contract known as *Least Cost, Technically Acceptable*. In this type of contract, vendors expend the absolute minimum of time, effort, and resources to just barely meet the requirements of the contract. This is the type of contract that is responsible for useless telephone support lines at government agencies and that implausibly thin "toilet paper" found in park restrooms. When it comes to your relationship with the Lord, there is no such thing as *Least Cost, Technically Acceptable*. Just as teachers look for continuous effort and growth in their students, so God looks for continuous effort and growth in your spiritual life. He looks for this not for his own benefit, but because he knows that your life will be blessed through this process.

Matthew chapters 19 & 20 tell of a person coming to Jesus asking: *Teacher, what good deed must I do to have eternal life?* Jesus went on to tell one of a number of parables that help us to understand that God does not have a fixed ruleset or criteria for getting rewards in heaven. In what has become known as *The Parable of the Laborers in the Vineyard*, he tells of a farmer who hired day laborers–some towards the end of the day, and some early in the morning. The ones who were hired latest in the day had little time to do much, while the ones hired earliest in the morning had all day to work. Both received the same reward. As Jesus hung on the cross, a thief hanging next to him put his faith in Christ (Luke 23:39-43). This man's life was at an end and he had little opportunity to do more than utter a few kind words to Jesus. The man, like the day laborer hired toward the end of the day, was given his reward–Jesus assured him: *Truly, I say to you, today you will be with me in Paradise.* As you read this book, it is likely that your life is more analogous to the day laborer hired in the earlier part of the day. You have time to build your prayer life, build your people skills, overcome your fears, grow your compassion, and share the love of Christ with many around you.

In *The Parable of the Talents,* (Matthew 25:14-30), Jesus tells a story of a master who entrusts his servants with various amounts of money to invest. In this parable, Christ explains that those who used these resources productively were rewarded, while those who didn't were rejected and thrown out. Jesus was trying to get across two clear messages with this teaching. The first is that we are all different and, therefore, we cannot compare ourselves with others. What God expects from you may be quite different from what he expects from me; we have all been endowed with a different set of resources. The second is that, whatever the resources, God expects us to find a way to increase them–to expand our capacity for love.

Interestingly, many Christians fall victim to two pitfalls once they have been living in a manner that has leveraged the principles and ideas that have been shared in this book. The first pitfall is that they fail to realize that their resources have grown. That is, when we first come to truly know the heart of Christ, it is likely that we don't know how to pray, we don't know how to help people, and we may not be particularly good at providing compassionate comfort. As the years go by, we continue to see ourselves as people who aren't good at these things. It is important to realize that each day you are gaining new life and, therefore, each day you need to set aside your fears and step out a little further than you were able to on the previous days. I am convinced that the most painful words that Christ ever hears are "I can't" and "I won't." God sent his son and built his church so that we could be filled with his knowledge and surrounded with the support we need so that we can and we will.

The second major pitfall, one that is a particular stumbling block for older Christians is the notion that it's OK to plateau–that it's OK to stop growing and stretching and serving once you reach some sort of Christian retirement age. If you reach a point in your spiritual walk when you cannot remember the last time that you stepped outside your comfort zone, the last time you reached out to someone who doesn't know the love of Christ and helped them to feel it, the last time you learned something new from God's word and felt excited about how you might apply the knowledge, then you may have fallen into Christian retirement. We have many ways in which we can share the love of God. It may be that a rock-climbing ministry is no longer an option for you, but it is likely that you could help host a small group, offer to teach a cooking class to young mothers, or spend time visiting lonely people in nursing homes, jails, or hospitals. The need for love, friendship, kindness, and compassion in the world is real, and God is looking to you to help fill this void.

God is not excited about someone who simply wants to *get into heaven*, someone who thinks that heaven is a place made for their pampering. God is excited about everyone who wants a relationship with him *now* because they love his love and they want to share his love with all those around them.

All this talk of personal growth may seem like an extra burden on an already busy and stressful life but, in reality, quite the opposite is true. Growing closer to the Lord and building friendships with, and serving beside, other Christians will reduce life's stresses and bring more fulfillment, happiness, and joy into your life. Jesus understood how hard life can be, so he made us this offer: *Come to me, all who labor and are heavy laden, and I will give you rest. Take my yoke upon you, and learn from me, for I am gentle and lowly in heart, and you will find rest for your souls. For my yoke is easy, and*

God Worthy?

my burden is light. (Matthew 11:28-30.)

Reiterating what was said at the start of this book, there is no set formula for strengthening your relationship with God. Even the most talented theologian cannot put God in a box. You need to listen to God, learn from God, trust God, love God and, most importantly, you need to do these every day, for if you do, then surely you will be worthy of God.

❧

God Worthy?, as the introduction indicated, provides a short course in Christianity through the lens of three important questions: *Am I worthy of God?*, *What does it mean to live a life worthy of God?*, and *Is God worthy of you?* But to this point, has only indirectly addressed the last of these. Some may believe that it is heretical to ask such a question, but it is, in fact, a very important question to ask. In the world today, many people follow many gods (or at least their notion of a god) and, in the course of this following, have hurt others and hurt themselves. To answer the question, *Is God worthy of you?*, we must first ask, *what does it mean for a god to be worthy?* In our culture today, people idolize those that are powerful, wealthy, attractive, or popular. In athletics, we are fans of the best players, in entertainment (and in the pulpit) we support the most attractive stars, and in business and politics, we support the wealthiest and those whose name we hear most. Is it wise to utilize these same criteria when deciding to follow a god?

The God of Abraham, Isaac, and Jacob is all-powerful, but when he arrived on this planet to begin building his church, he arrived as a child of peasants. Even when he did demonstrate power, he frequently instructed those around him to keep quiet about this display as we find in Mark 7:36: *And Jesus charged them to tell no one.* God gave instructions on the construction of the tabernacle but did

Conclusion

not have the Israelites carve an image of him. The Bible, with all its rich literary detail, contains no description of Jesus' physical appearance other than a prophetic reference in Isaiah 53:2 *he had no form or majesty that we should look at him, and no beauty that we should desire him.* Within the text of the Gospels, the only mention of Jesus owning anything is in John 19:23 where we learn that he owned an outfit: *When the soldiers had crucified Jesus, they took his garments and divided them into four parts, one part for each soldier; also his tunic.* Finally, when large crowds started to follow him, rather than preach to increase his popularity, Jesus preached tough words and, as recorded in John 6:60, *After this many of his disciples turned back and no longer walked with him.* In fact, Acts 1:15 records that only about 120 disciples remained together after the crucifixion.

If the standard by which we judge a god is power, wealth, good looks, or popularity, then it appears that Christ has no interest in scoring high in our evaluation. In John 13:35, Jesus says to his disciples, *By this all people will know that you are my disciples, if you have love for one another.* From this verse, we see that the primary attribute that Jesus wants to be known for is love. The Bible story reveals that God has great affection for us. The Gospels demonstrate that God was willing to conform his nature to ours, in the person of Christ, so that we can understand this love. The story of God's redemptive plan, from Noah to Jesus, illuminates the depth of his love for us, and the gift of the Holy Spirit, which provides us a new life with him, testifies to the power of his love. As you stand back and ponder the entire history of man's relationship with the Lord, you realize that God loves us with all his heart, soul, mind, and strength. God loves us so much that he has given us free will and given us comfort when we have misused this free will. He has given us wisdom, which brings about joy and happiness through his Holy Word and he has built up a church to seek us out and guide us back into a living relationship with him. As the prophet

God Worthy?

Micah said: *Who is a God like you?*

Whether we accept God as worthy of us or not is a decision everyone ultimately has to make for themselves. Will you choose to accept this God who loves you both like a father and a brother, and who offers you a peace that will surpass all understanding, through his son Jesus Christ, as worthy of you?

ACKNOWLEDGMENTS

A special thanks to Henry, Kenny, Wayne, Joe, Will, Gary, Mitchell, and Mom for their invaluable insight, Marla for her support in editing, and my wife and family for their support of this project.